D0017056

TAKING BACK AMERICA

TAKING

BACK ▬▬▬

AMERICA

AND TAKING DOWN
THE RADICAL RIGHT

EDITED BY
KATRINA VANDEN HEUVEL
AND ROBERT L. BOROSAGE

NATION BOOKS
NEW YORK

TAKING BACK AMERICA: *And Taking Down the Radical Right*

Compilation Copyright © 2004 by Katrina vanden Heuvel
and Robert L. Borosage

Published by
Nation Books
An Imprint of Avalon Publishing Group
245 West 17th St., 11th Floor
New York, NY 10011

Nation Books is a co-publishing venture of the Nation Institute and
Avalon Publishing Group Incorporated.

All rights reserved. No part of this publication may be reproduced or
transmitted in any form or by any means, electronic or mechanical,
including photocopy, recording, or any information storage and
retrieval system now known or to be invented, without permission in
writing from the publisher, except by a reviewer who wishes to quote
brief passages in connection with a review written for inclusion in a
magazine, newspaper, or broadcast.

Library of Congress Cataloging-in-Publication Data is available.

ISBN 1-56025-583-8

9 8 7 6 5 4 3 2 1

Book design by Simon M. Sullivan

Printed in the United States of America
Distributed by Publishers Group West

*For citizens across the country who
are building the new progressive majority*

TABLE OF CONTENTS

INTRODUCTION
Take Back America
By Katrina vanden Heuvel
and Robert L. Borosage

AMERICA HAS SUFFERED A staggering decline in its fortunes over the past three years. We've fallen from prosperity to recession and "recovery" without jobs. We've gone from peace to war, from relief at the end of the Cold War to fear at the hand of terrorists. We've experienced the worst corporate scandals in a century, the worst stock market collapse ever, the most glaring inequality since the Gilded Age. The federal budget has gone from record surplus to record deficit, while we keep adding to the largest foreign debt on record. The states are still struggling with the worst fiscal crisis in fifty years.

America's families are paying the price. Even with the economy officially "in recovery," wages are down and unemployment is up. Health care is broken. Millions have had their dreams for retirement shattered. Children are victimized as teachers get laid off, classrooms grow more crowded, and preschool and afterschool programs are discontinued. College tuitions are soaring, pricing more and more young people out of the education they deserve.

Instead of addressing those challenges, the policies of the Bush administration are part of the problem. Selected for office by the conservative majority of the Supreme Court after losing the popular vote, Bush has pursued a radical-right agenda remarkably divorced from what he campaigned on—pre-emptive war; destabilizing tax cuts; radical court packing; relentless rollback of protections for workers, consumers, and the environment; assault on the rights of women and minorities; and a crony capitalist corruption devoid even of shame.

Surely, it is time for progressives to rouse themselves, to build the arguments, movements, and institutions needed to turn this country around. It is time to take back America. While many translate this into electoral terms—defeating Bush in 2004—it is more than a matter of one election or changing occupants of the White House. It requires a coherent challenge to the conservative ideas that have dominated the past twenty-five years. It requires both bold new thought and new citizen mobilization to counter the entrenched and growing power of the lobbies for corporations and private wealth. It is a journey not of a year, but of a decade or more.

This book arises largely from an opening salvo in that effort—the extraordinary gathering of progressives convened in mid-2003 by the Campaign for America's Future. More than 2,000 participants—activists from unions, civil rights groups, the women's movement, the environmental lobby, the religious community—joined to share ideas and strategy. Leading public scholars laid out core elements of an agenda to challenge the current course. Activists detailed new institutions and strategies—from the Web action of MoveOn.org to the ground work of Americans Coming Together—to mobilize, energize, register, and engage Americans. And in accepting an award for his remarkable independent journalism, Bill Moyers delivered a dramatic address that put the current moment in historic perspective. In this reader, we've updated many of the presentations made at the conference and added seminal articles from *The Nation* magazine and elsewhere. This introduction summarizes the larger argument made by this collection.

I. THE CONSERVATIVE TRIUMPH AND FAILURE

Political analysts depict America as a country divided politically. The two major parties are about even in avowed partisan support. The 2000 presidential election was one of the closest in history, with Gore winning the popular vote by only 500,000 votes. The Senate and Congress are closely divided; so too are state governments, with the parties splitting almost evenly everything from the governorships to the state legislatures. Two Americas, the "red states and blue states," the secular against the religious, the North against the South, the party of white sanctuary against the party of the melting pot—the divisions are drawn repeatedly.

But beneath this divide, the past twenty-five years have been dominated by a conservative era, first ushered into preeminence by Ronald Reagan in 1980. Democratic majorities in Congress and Bill Clinton in the White House embraced many of the themes of that era—small government, tax cuts, deregulation, free trade, privatization. Clinton's sporadic efforts to revive a more progressive government ran aground on the Gingrich takeover of Congress and the relentless right-wing assault on his presidency. So, as William Grieder outlines, even with the Congress virtually divided between the parties, George W. Bush—with neither popular mandate nor popular majority—has been able to push through a remarkably reactionary agenda.

Today in Washington, the self-described "movement conservatives" that have dominated the politics of the past two decades have never been more powerful or more bankrupt. They dominate the Republican Party in both houses of Congress and drive the policies of the Bush administration, yet they have no credible answers to the new challenges that America faces.

President Bush's general response to the decline in American fortunes is to duck responsibility—the "no fault" president. He argues that he is not responsible, but merely a hapless victim of events. And to some extent, he is right. The president did not cause September 11, or the recession, or the bursting of the stock market bubble, or the corporate scandals. The trade deficit has been growing in good times and bad.

But it is increasingly clear that the conservative agenda is part of the problem, not part of the solution. The conservative reforms of the past years have contributed directly to our present condition. They deregulated financial markets, freeing up corporations and capital. The result has left the U.S. as the world's largest debtor and forged a global economy marked by greater instability and inequality, and dependent upon unsustainable U.S. trade deficits. They cut taxes on the wealthy and raised burdens on working families. They weakened the cop on the corporate beat and touted the cult of the CEO, opening the way for the corporate crime wave that has sapped investor confidence. Conservatives waged an unrelenting war against unions, trampling the right to organize and strike. They've unraveled the safety net, while blocking increases in the minimum wage. Now CEO salaries reach 500 times the wage of a full-time worker, while families work longer hours—longer even than the Japanese once famous for their work ethic—and yet find health care, tuitions, and retirement security increasingly unaffordable. Conservatives have fought against environmental regulation while denying the global threat posed by despoliation. They've labored to roll back affirmative action, stymie progress on equal rights, and take away women's right to choose.

For Americans, of course, the question is not one of blame, but of solution. How do we ensure a better America for our children? President Bush and the conservative leaders of Congress, Sen. Bill Frist and Rep. Tom DeLay, chant only the same, tired mantra—smaller government, lower taxes, deregulation, a strong military, traditional values. But our government is already the smallest of the industrial world, our taxes the lowest, our military the strongest. The policies and postures that got us into this fix are not likely to get us out. They are part of the problem, not part of the solution.

The failures of the Bush administration provide ample evidence. This administration has handed large swaths of policy to the most extreme ideologues of the right. Its foreign policy has been given over to the neoconservatives who trumpet preemptive war and a new American empire. Its fiscal policy is guided by zealots who use tax cuts to sap the capacity of government to act. Its judicial nominees are vetted by Federalist Society extremists who seek activist judges to overturn half a century of jurisprudence and cripple the authority of the government to regulate corporations and to protect consumers, workers, and the environment. Its attorney general claims the right to arrest American citizens and hold them indefinitely, without charges, without a lawyer, without a hearing. No wonder he put a shroud over the statue of Lady Justice.

For American families, the policies of Bush, Frist, and DeLay simply make things worse.

Wages are not keeping up, and good jobs are getting harder to find. But Bush's economic policy of high-end tax cuts created the largest deficit in history while producing more jobs in Shanghai than in Saginaw. He will end his term with the worst jobs record of any president since Herbert Hoover and the Great Depression. His corporate trade policies continue to drive manufacturing jobs overseas, while doing nothing to address the unsustainable trade imbalance. His opposition to the minimum wage and systematic efforts to weaken labor unions only exacerbate inequality and widen the gulf between CEO and worker.

Soaring health care costs leave millions uninsured, and many more a serious illness away from ruin. States are closing nursing homes and cutting back on children's health care. Prescription drug prices—the highest in the world—force seniors to go without the medicine they need. Yet Bush, Frist, and DeLay have no plan to deal with health care costs, much less the rising number of Americans with no health insurance. They fought against helping the states deal with soaring Medicaid costs. And in a brazen payoff to the drug companies that spent millions campaigning for Republicans in the last election, the president's prescription drug plan actually prohibits Medicare from negotiating the best price for seniors. They have effectively turned the $400 billion prescription drug bill into a subsidy for drug companies rather than a benefit for seniors.

The stock market collapse shattered the retirement plans of millions of working Americans. Only one in two workers even has a savings plan at work. Companies are rolling back guaranteed pensions, forcing workers into private savings plans, and slashing corporate contributions in the switch. Yet Bush, Frist, and DeLay push legislation that makes it easier to reward the top floor and ignore the shop floor. They offer the affluent greater ways to save tax-free, but have no plan to help the working families that survive paycheck to paycheck. Despite opposition by majorities in both houses of Congress, the president insisted on regulations that will strip millions of workers to the right to a forty-hour week with overtime pay. The president's "ownership society" will add to U.S. inequality by increasing tax burdens on salaries while exempting the investment income of the wealthy from taxes. And his plan to privatize Social Security would cut its guaranteed benefits, turning it from a program of shared security to one of individual risk.

Americans are sending the largest wave of children into our public schools since the baby boom after World War II. The schools are overcrowded and under-repaired. And they face the largest wave of teacher retirements ever. College tuitions and costs are being hiked across the country, and more and more students are forced by finances to forgo the education they have earned.

The federal government spends only two percent of its budget on public schools, yet Bush, Frist, and DeLay oppose any significant increase. The president pledges to build schools in Iraq but blocks construction funds at home. He even broke his promise to fund his own education reforms. His current budget offers no hope for making preschool universal, while it scrimps on afterschool programs. Under his budget, college loans and scholarships will fall further behind rising costs. A president who cuts taxes on millionaires while teachers are being laid off across the country is turning his back on the future.

And when it comes to making Americans safer, the administration's policies are wanting. The president earned the gratitude of the nation for leading the U.S. military against al Qaeda bases in Afghanistan, and the gratitude of most Iraqis, however fleeting, for toppling Saddam Hussein. But Bush's policy of pre-emptive war and unilateral intervention overturns fifty years of bipartisan policy; it has isolated America abroad, squandering the good will that followed September 11; and has made the United States an even greater target of terrorist rage. His occupation of Iraq places American forces at risk in a mission for which they have neither training nor appetite. And at home, the president has put tax cuts before the investments vital to bolstering our defenses against terror—in public health monitoring systems, in protection of our ports, and in defense plans for chemical and nuclear plants whose destruction could kill thousands.

Jobs, wages and benefits, retirement security, health care, education, even the safety of Americans—conservative policies are part of the problem, not part of the solution. It is hard to recall an administration more out of tune with the needs of the time. We need to go another way.

II. THE PROGRESSIVE CHALLENGE

The conservative failure opens both opportunity and imperative for a progressive revival, based on new priorities and a new agenda. The principles of a common-sense progressive reform agenda are clear. Put people first. A government on your side. Invest in America. Fair taxes and shared sacrifice. Hold corporations accountable. Empower workers and reward work. Secure families. Equal opportunity and a fair start for all. Defend America in a dangerous world. The readings we present gather some of America's finest public scholars to outline policies priorities for today.

Put America Back to Work

America works when Americans work. As we learned at the end of the Clinton years, in a full-employment economy, wages rise across the board, and the blessings of prosperity are spread, with resources generated for vital public and private investments.

Conservatives now proclaim victory for the program of top-end tax cuts, as the economy starts to grow. But with the Federal Reserve holding interest rates at record lows, with record deficits from soaring spending and sumptuous top-end tax cuts, and with the dollar losing some 40 percent to the euro in three years, it would have been impossible for the economy not to grow. Conservatives have only proven Keynes right: Government action can make a difference.

But the Bush "program" is surely the least efficient and most destabilizing way to get the economy going. James Galbraith and Robert Reich outline both a critique of the Bush agenda and elements of a sensible alternative. Their basic theme is that trickledown economics doesn't work. A far more efficient program for economic recovery and sustained long-term growth is to invest in areas vital to our future. Build schools, repair sewers, extend roads, invest in public health and homeland security. Add to that aid to the states for schools, teachers, health care and frontline defense. For an immediate stimulus, tax cuts should be temporary, not permanent, and aimed at middle- and lower-income Americans more likely to spend the money they receive than the wealthy who, by definition, already spend as much as they choose.

We need a new long-term growth economics that generates demand from the bottom up, lifting wages and benefits for working people. This requires empowering workers to gain a fair share of the productivity gains they produce. Start by making the right to organize and bargain collectively a core civil right, exposing and cracking down on illegal corporate strategies to crush union organizing and to eviscerate the right to strike. Empower a majority of workers to sign membership cards to create a union, without having to endure employer intimidation tactics in a skewed election. We should raise the minimum wage so that a full-time worker can pull a family out of poverty.

Capture the Future:
An Apollo Program for Energy Independence

As Bracken Hendriks discusses, one centerpiece of a progressive economic-reform agenda should be a program for energy independence. Hendriks argues for an initiative with the urgency and scope of John F. Kennedy's original Apollo program that put a man on the moon—a $300 billion, ten-year plan to invest in hybrid cars, renewable energy, efficient buildings and appliances, and diversified transit. This will turn a national security imperative into an economic opportunity, helping U.S. workers and companies capture the markets of the future. It will generate more jobs than the president's tax cuts at a fraction of the cost. And at the same time, it will make investments we vitally need to reduce our dependence on Persian Gulf oil. And it will enable us to rejoin the global effort to meet the threat posed by global warming.

The Right to a High Quality Public Education

Robert L. Borosage and Earl Hadley call on progressives to champion education reform. A central reason America has prospered and its democracy has thrived is that it has led the world in public education. Americans were the first to require twelve years of school for all. And the first to open higher education to the children of middle- and low-income families. Now our commitment to a high-quality public education for every child must be renewed.

Every school dollar must be used effectively. This requires continued efforts to reform schools, to raise standards, to reduce inefficiency, to cut layers of bureaucratic administration. At the same time, we need to invest enough to guarantee the right to a high-quality public education to every child. With both parents working, this should include quality preschool education and afterschool programs. We need to invest in building new schools, recruiting new teachers, and reducing class size. We cannot let college education be priced out of the reach of working families. Loan and grant programs should be expanded so that every child can afford all the education that they have earned with their achievements.

The Right to Affordable Health Care

The centerpiece of any reform agenda—and the center of

American concerns around the kitchen table—is affordable, high-quality health care. Robert Kuttner outlines strategies for reviving this demand in the political debate. Ironically, high-quality health care for all Americans is not a matter of more money. We already spend more of our GDP on health care than other industrial countries who provide for all their citizens. Yet every year some 75 million Americans go without health insurance, and soaring costs are pricing adequate insurance out of reach of seniors, workers, small businesses, and large corporations. The question is how to overcome the entrenched resistance by powerful special interests and perfervid conservative opponents. As Kuttner argues, surely the first step is to bite the bullet and put the issue back on the political agenda.

A Secure Retirement

Guaranteed retirement security at the end of a life of work was a triumph of the twentieth century, but now it is under assault. Half of all workers have no pension plan at work. Corporations are turning guaranteed pensions into individualized savings plans, and slashing corporate contributions in the process. As the Enron workers found out, the gulf between the top floor and the shop floor has grown, with executives getting ever more lavish retirement packages while workers are denied control of their own savings plans, if they have one. And now the president wants to privatize Social Security and turn that into an individual risk plan while masking deep cuts in government contributions.

Progressives should work to provide workers with the opportunity for retirement security. That requires bolstering Social

Security and defending it from those who would privatize it while slashing guaranteed benefits. It requires reform of America's pension system in an economy where workers move from job to job. Pension coverage should be mandatory, as should be a minimal employer contribution. The government should subsidize a basic minimum of savings for low- and moderate-income workers. Workers should be given a voice in the placement of their own retirement savings. Without a serious reorientation of our retirement policy, we will continue spending more than $100 billion in forgone tax revenue to subsidize a system that fails the majority of households. The estimated $45 billion annual cost to the federal government of this new initiative is manageable, and can be financed simply by reversing the added tax breaks offered the wealthiest Americans in the Bush tax plan.

A Healthy Environment

As Deb Callahan argues, clean air, clean water, and safe food are necessities, not luxuries. Every year, millions of Americans suffer costly illness; thousands even die, from unsafe and untested food. Global warming, oceans in peril, and toxic waste cannot be ignored. Corporate self-regulation has been shown to fail. We need to strengthen food safety, workplace safety, and environmental protection programs, not weaken them. We should make polluters pay for the toxic wastes that they generate, while ensuring that citizens have the right to know about the threats to their environment posed by local plants. And rather than simply abandoning the Kyoto protocol on global warming, we should be leading the world in forging the policies needed to reduce emissions while moving toward sustainable growth.

A Secure America

Making Americans safe in a world marked by increasing inequality, instability, and terrorism with a global reach is no easy task. This administration has rallied the country to fight wars in Afghanistan and Iraq in the wake of September 11. But military prowess alone offers no adequate response. Terrorism is the weapon of the weak, what the military terms an "asymmetrical" response to overwhelming military power. "Shock and awe," as we are already learning in Iraq, is not its solution but its spur.

In two thoughtful articles, Tom Andrews and Benjamin Barber lay out both a critique of the Bush policy of pre-emptive war and elements of an alternative agenda. The debacle in Iraq has demonstrated both how prescient their arguments are and how pressing the need for an alternative is.

Clearly, progressives must champion a real security policy that will help make America safe. This requires not unilateralism, but a renewed and muscular internationalism, working to forge a global consensus against terrorism, and to wage an unrelenting global campaign to isolate terrorist groups and bring their leaders to justice. This requires building alliances, developing international institutions and international law, and global efforts to share the burdens of enforcement and to provide legitimacy at home and abroad. We need active diplomacy to lead global efforts to bring peace and security to explosive hot spots like the Middle East. And we should enlist others in helping to build a more just world, to fight devastating plagues and poverty, to spread the blessings of public health and education, to open the opportunity for growth and democracy. As Andrews argues,

America will be more secure if it makes itself a source of hope, not of fear.

At home, September 11 was said to change everything. But it did not alter the Bush administration's fixation on annual tax breaks for the wealthy, which have taken precedence even over basic investments in homeland security—guarding our ports and most deadly plants, rebuilding our impoverished public health care system, creating an early warning system for biological or chemical assaults, and subsidizing hard-pressed localities for the cost of greater front-line protections. Progressives must overcome the radical antigovernment animus of the right that is now impeding essential investments that will make Americans safer.

Affording the Future

Can we afford to invest in the future? The simple answer is that we cannot afford not to. America is a wealthy country, blessed with remarkable resources. The question is not one of money but of priorities.

Today our deficits still are proportionately among the lowest in the industrialized world. If we embrace a new economic course, we can afford the investments we need in the future. Faster economic growth will generate greater resources and lower burdens. Attempts to eliminate deficits through austerity without comprehensive health care reform are futile, leading to slower growth and larger deficits that require further cuts.

New priorities can free up literally hundreds of billions of dollars. Corporate subsidies and tax breaks—many of them without any redeeming public purpose—waste tens of billions of dollars a year. With the Pentagon budget expanding in reaction to September 11, we are spending almost as much on our military as the rest of the world combined, wasting billions in an arms race with ourselves.

Even then, the radical effort to cripple government by lowering taxes, primarily on the wealthy, must be stopped. Today, taxes are scheduled to go down to levels not seen since the Eisenhower era, before Medicare and Medicaid. If this is not reversed, we will not only be unable to make investments in education vital to our future, we won't be able to afford Medicare and Social Security, core guarantees that one generation makes to the next. Fairer, simple, and progressive taxes—reversing the regressive tax changes and closing the loopholes of the past decades—are essential, and can also generate new resources, even while sustaining the lowest tax rates in the industrial world.

At the end of almost two decades of conservative "tax breaks" America's wealthiest investor, Warren Buffett, reports that he is paying about the same percentage of his income in taxes as his secretary does. The Bush drive to eliminate taxes on unearned income—capital gains and dividends—will increase the burden on workers, Buffett warns, and his secretary will end up paying a higher percentage in taxes than he does. He calls this "class welfare for the affluent." It has no justification at a time when inequality is at record levels and virtually all of the benefits of economic growth flow to the wealthiest 20 percent of Americans. Progressive tax reform—one that taxes people according to their ability to pay—is long overdue. In a time of growing inequality, we should be lowering tax burdens on low-income workers and raising them on the affluent. And we should tax corporate behavior that we want to discourage—such as short-term financial speculation or offshore tax havens.

Empower Citizens

Any significant change in our national direction will require a movement to empower citizens and curb the influence of big-money special interests. Bush, Frist, and DeLay have shamelessly provided access, special treatment, inside deals, and no-bid contracts to those who pay for their parties. Billions of public dollars are leeched off for private purposes.

As Miles Rapoport argues, progressives must lead a national effort to clean up Washington, to curb the influence of money in politics, to expand the ability of candidates to present their case to the American people without being forced into an unending money chase, and to mobilize citizens to take back their government. We will work to clean out the entrenched lobbies in Washington and to limit the revolving doors and double standards that transform public service into private wealth. The politics of money will only be dislodged by a new politics of citizen action and mobilization.

But political reform alone is not enough. As John Nichols and Robert W. McChesney suggest, progressives must challenge the increasing concentration of ownership in the media, even while aggressively developing the potential—merely glimpsed by the activities of MoveOn.org and the Howard Dean campaign—of independent communication through the World Wide Web.

Reviving democracy can most easily begin not at the national level which receives our attention, but at the state and local level. As Joel Rogers outlines, "devolve this" should be turned into a progressive rallying cry, not a conservative ploy. States and localities ought to be the laboratories in which new progressive reforms are shaped. The conservative strategy of devolution—cooked up by states' rights advocates seeking to limit the reforms of the civil rights movement and the New Deal—opens an opportunity that progressives should seize.

The Emerging Progressive Majority

Political eras come to an end when the dominant parties or ideologies are unable to address the needs of the time—challenges that are often unintended consequences of their own policies. By this measure, the movement represented by Reagan, Gingrich, Bush, Frist, and DeLay is exhausted.

But a political movement can sustain itself in power long after its intellectual bankruptcy is apparent. The regime of Bush, Frist, and DeLay is buttressed by a politics dominated by big money and special interests, embedded in a media ever more concentrated, cowed, or co-opted, and armed with a ruthless modern political machine that enforces its line, echoes its message, and assaults its critics. Bush has not hesitated to turn patriotism into a partisan club, and September 11 into a presidential prop. Republicans have learned to don liberal garb on issues where necessary—on prescription drugs, Social Security, and even corporate accountability. And special interests spend millions to help blur differences and discredit opponents.

The President enjoyed high poll ratings in the wake of the victory over Iraq. His Republican Party has perfected symbolic politics to appeal to social conservatives, while using the right-wing evangelicals as a ground operation to mobilize and register voters.

Republicans have consolidated their position as the party of white sanctuary in the South.

But the right increasingly looks not like a realigning majority, as the president's political guru, Karl Rove, would have us believe, but as a rearguard minority, arraying its entrenched prowess to forestall the rise of a majority movement.

On fundamental questions, Bush and the right are out of tune with the vast majority of Americans. In area after area, the majority of Americans prefer progressive alternatives to the failed policies of the conservative right—investment in health care and education over tax cuts, fair trade over free trade, corporate accountability over deregulation, environmental protection over laissez-faire policies, defending Social Security and Medicare over privatizing them, public schools over vouchers, raising the minimum wage over eliminating it. And civil rights, choice, environmental protection—the causes of the civilizing movements of the past decades are now mainstream values.

The outlines of a majority coalition for progressive reform have begun to emerge. It is built on the base of the Democratic Party—union workers, minorities, women, environmentalists. It appeals to non-college-educated, socially conservative voters with an economics that works for them, and it appeals to college educated, social liberals with a continued defense of basic values—education, civil rights, the environment, women's right to choose. It offers Americans a real security agenda that spurns the siren calls to a new American empire.

Skeptics suggest that conservatives have won the argument about public action, that the "era of big government is over," and that progressive support for investment in education or health care, calls for putting people to work and fair taxes, will be rejected by the American people. They urge that Democrats reposition themselves, with a focus on balancing the budget that rules out new initiatives that require major investments. They suggest that Democrats can win as fiscal conservatives with a liberal social agenda, fending off the extremes of the Republican Right.

This is bad policy and bad politics. The politics of duck and cover, position and pander, may steal an election, but they cannot change the direction of this country. Americans face real challenges that will not be addressed by the conservatives now in power. Progressives must champion their cause, and lay out an argument that makes sense. We must offer solutions that are commensurate with the size of the challenge. We must confront the failed conservative policies head-on, and expose the corruption and cronyism of the current regime

However, to challenge the right, progressives must have more than good ideas. We must build the independent capacity to reach out to citizens, to mobilize allies, to identify, recruit, train, and support the next generation of leaders.

But, as Jesse Jackson argues, it is vital now to come together, to bring the entire family together to meet the challenge posed by the right. Progressives would do well to learn from how the New Right responded to life in the political wilderness of the mid-1970s when Nixon was in disgrace and Democrats controlled everything. At that moment, New

Right strategists decided not to drift to the center, nor to start a third party. Instead they built independent institutions and independent capacity to drive their agenda, their values, and their movement into the political debate. They sought to take over the Republican Party from green-eye shade moderates and make it their vehicle. They built the Heritage Foundation, an openly right-wing propaganda center. They invested in the Moral Majority, galvanizing the right-wing evangelical movement. They built a network of conservative PACs, led by the National Conservative Political Action Committee. They mobilized a movement that transformed not only the Republican Party but the national political debate as well.

As Katrina vanden Heuvel argues, progressives must build the independent capacity to drive this energy into the political debate. In the run-up to 2004, this effort has begun. The Take Back America conference provides a strategy center for progressives, and challenges political candidates to speak clearly to a progressive agenda.

Jeff Blodgett describes the new Wellstone Action training center, which provides training for legions of organizers and activists for voter registration and mobilization projects, like those organized by the new Americans Come Together and America Votes.

Progressive Majority, as Gloria Totten describes, has created Propac, to recruit, train, and support the next generation of Paul Wellstones at the state and local level. Progressive Majority is also building a small donor network on the Web that can give early money to progressive challengers. The potential for this has been dramatized by MoveOn.org and the Howard Dean campaign. MoveOn.org is raising several million dollars from members over the Web, while creating a new politics of citizen engagement. And whatever happens in this election, when Howard Dean argued that he could counter the $200 million that George W. Bush would raise from his wealthy networks of "pioneers" with $200 million raised largely over the Web at $100 a pop, he broke the hold of Wall Street and big money on the money primary and heralded a new era of people politics.

The potential of that politics is apparent. Jeff Blodgett recalls the politics and passion of Paul Wellstone. His tragic death is an immeasurable loss both to those who knew him and to the progressive politics of our time. But he has left, as Jeff Blodgett notes, an example from which all can learn.

Paul understood clearly just how impoverished the Right was in ideas, even as they were buttressed by money and power. So he had little patience for those who suggested that we bite our tongues or trim our sails. It is time, as he said in one of his last speeches, not to duck, not to hide, not to bite our tongues, or bide our time. It is time to stand up, to speak out. To assert our values, our ideas, our energy. It is time to take back America.

TAKING BACK AMERICA

SECTION I

BUSH'S RADICAL REACTION

CHAPTER 1
The Threat

Although he campaigned as a moderate, "compassionate conservative," and took office without a mandate, having lost the popular vote, George W. Bush has pushed a remarkably aggressive reactionary agenda while in office. He has stocked his administration with ideologues, self-described "movement conservatives," and the extreme nature of his agenda at home and abroad has sparked increasing opposition. Here, The Nation's *national affairs correspondent, William Grieder, outlines the scope of the Right's ambition.*

ROLLING BACK THE TWENTIETH CENTURY*
by William Greider

I. BACK TO THE FUTURE

GEORGE W. BUSH, PROPERLY understood, represents the third and most powerful wave in the Right's long-running assault on the governing order created by twentieth-century liberalism. The first wave was Ronald Reagan, whose election in 1980 allowed movement conservatives finally to attain governing power (their flame was first lit by Barry Goldwater back in 1964). Reagan unfurled many bold ideological banners for right-wing reform and established the political viability of enacting regressive tax cuts, but he accomplished

*From *The Nation,* May 12, 2003

very little reordering of government, much less shrinking of it. The second wave was Newt Gingrich, whose capture of the House majority in 1994 gave Republicans control of Congress for the first time in two generations. Despite some landmark victories like welfare reform, Gingrich flamed out quickly, a zealous revolutionary ineffective as legislative leader.

George Bush II may be as shallow as he appears, but his presidency represents a far more formidable challenge than either Reagan or Gingrich. His potential does not emanate from an amiable personality (Al Gore, remember, outpolled him in 2000) or even the sky-high ratings generated by September 11 and war. Bush's governing strength is anchored in the long, hard-driving movement of the Right that now owns all three branches of the federal government. Its unified ranks allow him to govern aggressively, despite slender GOP majorities in the House and Senate and the public's general indifference to the Right's domestic program.

The movement's grand ambition—one can no longer say grandiose—is to roll back the twentieth century, quite literally. That is, defenestrate the federal government and reduce its scale and powers to a level well below what it was before the New Deal's centralization. With that accomplished, movement conservatives envision a restored society in which the prevailing values and power relationships resemble the America that existed around 1900, when William McKinley was president. Governing authority and resources are dispersed from Washington, returned to local levels and also to individuals and private institutions, most notably corporations and religious organizations. The primacy of private property rights is reestablished over the shared public priorities expressed in government regulation. Above all, private wealth—both enterprises and individuals with higher incomes—are permanently insulated from the progressive claims of the graduated income tax.

These broad objectives may sound reactionary and destructive (in historical terms they are), but hard-right conservatives see themselves as liberating reformers, not destroyers, who are rescuing old American virtues of self-reliance and individual autonomy from the clutches of collective action and "statist" left-wingers. They do not expect any of these far-reaching goals to be fulfilled during Bush's tenure, but they do assume that history is on their side and that the next wave will come along soon (not an unreasonable expectation, given their great gains during the past thirty years). Right-wingers—who once seemed frothy and fratricidal—now understand that three steps forward, two steps back still adds up to forward progress. It's a long march, they say. Stick together, because we are winning.

Many opponents and critics (myself included) have found the Right's historic vision so improbable that we tend to guffaw and misjudge the political potency of what it has put together. We might ask ourselves: If these ideas are so self-evidently cockeyed and reactionary, why do they keep advancing? The Right's unifying idea—get the government out of our lives—has broad popular appeal, at least on a sentimental level, because it represents an authentic core value in the American experience. ("Don't tread on me" was a slogan in the Revolution.) But the true source of its strength is the movement's fluid architecture and durability over time, not the passing personalities of Reagan-Gingrich-Bush or even the big money from business. The movement has a substantial base that believes in its ideological vision—people alarmed by cultural change or injured in some way by government intrusions, coupled with economic interests that have very strong reasons to get government off their backs—and the Right has created the political mechanics that allow these disparate elements to pull together. Cosmopolitan corporate executives hold their noses and go along with Christian activists trying to stamp out "decadent" liberal culture. Fed-up working-class conservatives support business's assaults on their common enemy, liberal government, even though they may be personally injured when business objectives triumph.

The Right's power also feeds off the general decay in the political system—the widely shared and often justifiable resentments felt toward big government, which no longer seems to address the common concerns of ordinary citizens. I am not predicting that the Right will win the governing majority that could enact the whole program, in a kind of right-wing New Deal—and I will get to some reasons why I expect their cause to fail eventually. The farther they advance, however, the less inevitable is their failure.

II. THE McKINLEY BLUEPRINT

In the months after last November's elections, the Bush administration rattled progressive sensibilities with shock and awe on the home front—a barrage of audacious policy initiatives: Allow churches to include sanctuaries of worship in buildings financed by federal housing grants. Slash hundreds of billions in domestic programs, especially spending for the poor, even as the Bush tax cuts kick in for the well-to-do.

At the behest of Big Pharma, begin prosecuting those who help the elderly buy cheaper prescription drugs in Canada. Compel the District of Columbia to conduct federally financed school voucher experiments (even though DC residents are overwhelmingly opposed). Reform Medicaid by handing it over to state governments, which will be free to make their own rules, much like welfare reform. Do the same for housing aid, food stamps, and other long-established programs. Redefine "wetlands" and "wilderness" so that millions of protected acres are opened for development.

Liberal activists gasped at the variety and dangerous implications (the public might have been upset, too, but was preoccupied with war), while conservatives understood that Bush was laying the foundations, step by step, toward their grand transformation of American life. These are the concrete elements of their vision:

- Eliminate federal taxation of private capital, as the essential predicate for dismantling the progressive income tax. This will require a series of reform measures (one of them, repeal of the estate tax, is already accomplished). Bush has proposed several others: elimination of the tax on stock dividends and establishment of new tax-sheltered personal savings accounts for the growing "investor class." Congress appears unwilling to swallow these, at least this year, but their introduction advances the education-agitation process. Future revenue would be harvested from a single-rate flat tax on wages or, better still, a stiff sales tax on consumption. Either way, labor gets taxed, but not capital. The 2003 Economic Report of the President, prepared by the Council of Economic Advisers, offers a primer on the advantages of a consumption tax and how it might work. Narrowing the tax base naturally encourages smaller government.

- Gradually phase out the pension-fund retirement system as we know it, starting with Social Security privatization but moving eventually to breaking up the other large pools of retirement savings, even huge public-employee funds, and converting them into individualized accounts. Individuals will be rewarded for taking personal responsibility for their retirement with proposed "lifetime savings" accounts where capital is stored, forever tax-exempt. Unlike IRAs, which provide a tax deduction for contributions, wages are taxed upfront but permanently tax-sheltered when deposited as "lifetime" capital savings, including when the money is withdrawn and spent. Thus, this new format inevitably threatens the present system, in which employers get a tax deduction for financing pension funds for their workers. The new alternative should eventually lead to repeal of the corporate tax deduction and thus relieve business enterprise of any incentive to finance pensions for employees. Everyone takes care of himself.

- Withdraw the federal government from a direct role in housing, health care, assistance to the poor, and many other long-established social priorities, first by dispersing program management to local and state governments or private operators, then by steadily paring down the federal government's financial commitment. If states choose to kill an aid program rather than pay for it themselves, that confirms that the program will not be missed. Any slack can be taken up by the private sector, philanthropy, and especially religious institutions that teach social values grounded in faith.

- Restore churches, families, and private education to a more influential role in the nation's cultural life by giving them a significant new base of income—public money. When "school choice" tuitions are fully available to families, all taxpayers will be compelled to help pay for private school systems, both secular and religious, including Catholic parochial schools. As a result, public schools will likely lose some of their financial support, but their enrollments are expected to shrink anyway, as some families opt out. Although the core of Bush's "faith-based initiative" stalled in Congress, he is advancing it through new administrative rules. The voucher strategy faces many political hurdles, but the Supreme Court is out ahead, clearing away the constitutional objections.

- Strengthen the hand of business enterprise against burdensome regulatory obligations, especially environmental protection, by introducing voluntary goals and "market-driven" solutions. These will locate the decision-making on how much progress is achievable within corporate managements rather than enforcement agencies (an approach also championed in this year's Economic Report). Down the road, when a more aggressive right-wing majority is secured for the Supreme Court, conservatives expect to throw a permanent collar around the regulatory state by enshrining a radical new constitutional doctrine. It would require government to compensate private property owners, including businesses, for new regulations that impose costs on them or injure their profitability, a formulation sure to guarantee far fewer regulations.

- Smash organized labor. Though unions have lost considerable influence, they remain a major obstacle to achieving the Right's vision. Public-employee unions are formidable opponents on issues like privatization and school vouchers. Even the declining industrial unions still have the resources to mobilize a meaningful counterforce in politics. Above all, the labor movement embodies the progressives' instrument of power: collective action. The mobilization of citizens in behalf of broad social demands are inimical to the Right's vision of autonomous individuals, in charge of their own affairs and acting alone. Unions may be taken down by a thousand small cuts, like stripping "homeland security" workers of union protection. They will be more gravely weakened if pension funds, an enduring locus of labor power, are privatized.

Looking back over this list, one sees many of the old peevish conservative resentments—Social Security, the income tax, regulation of business, labor unions, big government central-ized in Washington—that represent the great battles that con-servatives lost during early decades of the twentieth century. That is why the McKinley era represents a lost Eden the right has set out to restore. Grover Norquist, president of Ameri-cans for Tax Reform and a pivotal leader in the movement's inside-outside politics, confirms this observation. "Yes, the McKinley era, absent the protectionism," he agrees, is the goal. "You're looking at the history of the country for the first 120 years, up until Teddy Roosevelt, when the socialists took over. The income tax, the death tax, regulation, all that." (In foreign policy, at least, the Bush administration could fairly be said to have already restored the spirit of that earlier age. Justifying the annexation of the Philippines, McKinley famously explained America's purpose in the world: "There was nothing left for us to do but to take them all, and to edu-cate the Filipinos, and uplift and civilize and Christianize them, and by God's grace do the very best we could by them, as our fellow men for whom Christ also died.")

But the Right employs a highly selective memory. McKinley Republicans, aligned with the newly emergent industrial titans, did indeed hold off the Progressive advo-cates of a federal income tax and other reforms, while its high tariffs were the equivalent of a stiff consumption tax. And its conservative Supreme Court blocked regulatory laws designed to protect society and workers as unconstitutional intrusions on private property rights.

But the truth is that McKinley's conservatism broke down not because of socialists but because a deeply troubled nation was awash in social and economic conflicts, inequities generated by industrialization and the awesome power consolidating in the behemoth industrial corporations (struggles not resolved until economic crisis spawned the New Deal). Reacting to popular demands, Teddy Roosevelt enacted landmark progressive reforms like the first federal regulations protecting public health and safety and a ban on corporate campaign contributions. Both Roosevelt and his successor, Republican William Howard Taft, endorsed the concept of a progressive income tax and other un-Republican measures later enacted under Woodrow Wilson.

George W. Bush does not, of course, ever speak of the glories of the McKinley era or acknowledge his party's retrograde objectives. Conservatives learned, especially from Gingrich's implosion, to avoid flamboyant ideological proclamations. Instead, the broader outlines are only hinted at in various official texts. But there's nothing really secretive about their intentions. Right-wing activists and think tanks have been openly articulating the goals for years. Some of their ideas that once sounded loopy are now law.

III. THE ECUMENICAL RIGHT

The movement "is moving with the speed of a glacier," explains Martin Anderson, a senior fellow at Stanford's Hoover Institution who served as Reagan's house intellectual, the keeper of the flame, and was among the early academics counseling George W. Bush. "It moves very slowly, stops sometimes, even retreats, but then it moves forward again. Sometimes, it comes up against a tree and seems stuck, then the tree snaps and people say, 'My gosh, it's a revolution.' " To continue the metaphor, Anderson thinks this glacier will run up against some big boulders that do not yield, that the Right will eventually be stopped short of grand objectives like small government or elimination of the income tax. But they've made impressive progress so far.

For the first time since the 1920s, Congress, the White House, and the Supreme Court are all singing from the same hymnal and generally reinforcing one another. The Court's right-wing majority acts to shrink federal authority, block citizen challenges of important institutions, and hack away at the liberal precedents on civil rights, regulatory law, and many other matters (it even decides an election for its side, when necessary).

Bush, meanwhile, has what Reagan lacked—a Reaganite majority in Congress. When the Gipper won in 1980, most Republicans in Congress were still traditional conservatives, not radical reformers. The majority of House Republicans tipped over to the Reaganite identity in 1984, a majority of GOP senators not until 1994. The ranks of the unconverted—Republicans who refuse to sign Norquist's pledge not to raise taxes—are now, by his count, down to 5 percent in the House caucus, 15 percent in the Senate.

This ideological solidarity is a central element in Bush's governing strength. So long as he can manage the flow of issues in accord with the big blueprint, the Right doesn't shoot at him when he makes politically sensitive deviations (import quotas for steel or the lavish new farm-subsidy bill). It also helps that, especially in the House, the GOP leaders impose Stalinist discipline on their troops. Bush also reassures the Far Right by making it clear that he is one of them. Reagan used to stroke the Christian Right with strong rhetoric on social issues but gave them very little else (the man was from Hollywood, after all). Bush is a true believer, a devout Christian, and exceedingly public about it. Bush's principal innovation—a page taken from Bill Clinton's playbook—is to confuse the opposition's issues by offering his own compassion-lite alternatives, co-opting or smothering Democratic initiatives. Unlike Clinton, Bush does not mollify his political base with empty gestures. Their program is his program.

"Reagan talked a good game on the domestic side but he actually didn't push for much," says Paul Weyrich, leader of the Free Congress Foundation and a movement pioneer. "Likewise, the Gingrich era was a lot of rhetoric. This administration is far more serious and disciplined . . . they have better outreach than any with which I have dealt. These people have figured out how to communicate regularly with their base, make sure it understands what they're doing. When they have to go against their base, they know how to inoculate themselves against what might happen."

Norquist's ambition is that building on its current strength, the Right can cut government by half over the next twenty-five years to "get it down to the size where we can drown it in the bathtub." The federal government would shrink from 20 percent of GDP to 10 percent, state and local government from 12 percent to 6 percent. When vouchers become universally available, he expects public schools to shrink from 6 percent to 3 percent of GDP. "And we'll have better schools," he assures. People like Norquist play the role of constantly pushing the boundaries of the possible. "I'm lining up support to abolish the alternative minimum tax," he says. "Has Bush spoken to this? No. I want to run ahead, put our guys on the record for it. So I will be out in front of the Bush administration, not attacking the Bush administration. Will he do everything we want? No, but you know what? I don't care."

Americans for Tax Reform serves as a kind of "action central" for a galaxy of conservative interests, with support from corporate names like Microsoft, Pfizer, AOL Time Warner, R. J. Reynolds, and the liquor industry. "The issue that brings people to politics is what they want from government," Norquist explains. "All our people want to be left alone by government. To be in this coalition, you only need to have your foot in the circle on one issue. You don't need a *Weltanschauung*, you don't have to agree with every other issue, so long as the coalition is right on yours. That's why we don't have the expected war within the center-right coalition. That's why we can win."

One of the Right's political accomplishments is bringing together diverse, once-hostile sectarians. "The Republican Party used to be based in the Protestant mainline and aggressively kept its distance from other religions," Norquist observes. "Now we've got observant Catholics, the people who go to mass every Sunday, evangelical Christians, Mormons, orthodox Jews, Muslims." How did it happen? "The secular Left has created an ecumenical Right," he says. This new tolerance, including on race, may represent meaningful social change, but of course the Right also still feeds on intolerance, too, demonizing those whose values or lifestyle or place of birth does not conform to their idea of "American."

This tendency, Norquist acknowledges, is a vulnerability. The swelling ranks of Latino and Asian immigrants could become a transforming force in American politics, once these millions of new citizens become confident enough to participate in election politics (just as European immigrants became a vital force for liberal reform in the early twentieth century). So Bush labors to change the party's anti-immigrant profile (and had some success with Mexican-Americans in Texas).

Norquist prefers to focus on other demographic trends that he believes insure the Right's eventual triumph: As the children of the New Deal die off, he asserts, they will be replaced by young "leave me alone" conservatives. Anderson, the former Reagan adviser, is less certain. "Most of the people like what government is doing," he observes. "So long as it isn't overintrusive and so forth, they're happy with it."

IV. Show Me the Money

Ideology may provide the unifying umbrella, but the real glue of this movement is its iron rule for practical politics: Every measure it enacts, every half-step it takes toward the grand vision, must deliver concrete rewards to one con- stituency or another, often several—and right now, not in the distant future. Usually the reward is money. There is nothing unusual or illegitimate about that, but it sounds like raw hypocrisy considering that the Right devotes enormous energy to denouncing "special-interest politics" on the Left (schoolteachers, labor unions, bureaucrats, Hollywood). The Right's interest groups, issue by issue, bring their muscle to the cause. Bush's "lifetime savings" accounts constitute a vast new product line for the securities industry, which is naturally enthused about marketing and managing these accounts. The terms especially benefit the well-to-do, since a family of four will be able to shelter up to $45,000 annually (that's more than most families earn in a year). The White House has enlisted Fortune 500 companies to spread the good news to the investor class in their regular mailings to shareholders.

Bush's "market-friendly" reforms for health care would reward two business sectors that many consumers regard as the problem—drug companies and HMOs. Big Pharma would get the best of all worlds: a federal subsidy for prescription drug purchases by the elderly, but without any limits on the prices. The insurance industry is invited to set up a privatized version of Medicare that would compete with the government-run system (assuming there are enough senior citizens willing to take that risk).

Some rewards are not about money. Bush has already provided a victory for "pro-lifers" with the ban on late-term abortions. The antiabortionists are realists now and no longer badger the GOP for a constitutional amendment, but perhaps a future Supreme Court, top-heavy with right-wing appointees, will deliver for them. Republicans are spoiling for a fight over guns in 2004, when the federal ban on assault rifles is due to expire. Liberals, they hope, will try to renew the law so the GOP can deliver a visible election-year reward by blocking it. (Gun-control advocates are thinking of forcing Bush to choose between the gun lobby and public opinion.)

The biggest rewards, of course, are about taxation, and the internal self-discipline is impressive. When Reagan proposed his huge tax-rate cuts in 1981, the K Street corporate lobbyists piled on their own list of goodies and the White House lost control; Reagan's tax cuts wound up much larger than he intended. This time around, business behaved itself when Bush proposed a tax package in 2001 in which its wish list was left out. "They supported the 2001 tax cuts because they knew there was going to be another tax cut every year and, if you don't support this year's, you go to the end of the line next time," Norquist says. Their patience has already been rewarded. The antitax movement follows a well-defined script for advancing step by step to the ultimate goal. Norquist has organized five caucuses to agitate and sign up congressional supporters on five separate issues: estate-tax repeal (already enacted but still vulnerable to reversal); retirement-savings reforms; elimination of the alternative minimum tax; immediate business deductions for capital investment expenses (instead of a multiyear depreciation schedule); and zero taxation of capital gains. "If we do all of these things, there is no tax on capital and we are very close to a flat tax," Norquist exclaims.

The road ahead is far more difficult than he makes it sound, because along the way a lot of people will discover that they are to be the losers. In fact, the McKinley vision requires vast sectors of society to pay dearly, and from their own pockets. Martin Anderson has worked through the flat-tax arithmetic many times, and it always comes out a political loser. "The conservatives all want to revolutionize the tax system, frankly because they haven't thought it through," Anderson says. "It means people from zero to $35,000 income pay no tax and anyone over $150,000 is going to get a tax cut. The people in between get a tax increase, unless you cut federal spending. That's not going to happen."

Likewise, any substantial consumption tax does severe injury to another broad class of Americans—the elderly. They were already taxed when they were young and earning and saving their money, but a new consumption tax would now tax their money again as they spend it. Lawrence Lindsey, Bush's former economic adviser, has advocated a consumption-based flat tax that would probably require a rate of 21 percent on consumer purchases (like a draconian sales tax). He concedes, "It would be hitting the current generation of elderly twice. So it would be a hard sell."

"School choice" is also essentially a money issue, though this fact has been obscured by the years of Republican rhetoric demonizing the public schools and their teachers. Under tuition vouchers, the redistribution of income will flow from all taxpayers to the minority of American families who send their children to private schools, religious and secular. Those children are less than 10 percent of the 52 million children enrolled in K–12. You wouldn't know it from reading about the voucher debate, but the market share of private schools actually declined slightly during the past decade. The Catholic parochial system stands to gain the most from public financing, because its enrollment has declined by half since the 1960s (to 2.6 million). Though there was some growth during the 1990s, it was in the suburbs, not cities. Other private schools, especially religious schools in the South, grew more during the past decade (by about 400,000), but public schools expanded far faster, by 6 million. The point is, the Right's constituency for "school choice" remains a small though fervent minority.

Conservatives have cleverly transformed the voucher question into an issue of racial equality—arguing that they are the best way to liberate impoverished black children from bad schools in slum surroundings. But educational quality notwithstanding, it is not self-evident that private schools, including the Catholic parochial system, are disposed to solve the problem of minority education, since they are highly segregated themselves. Catholic schools enroll only 2.5 percent of black students nationwide and, more telling, only 3.8 percent of Hispanic children, most of whom are Catholic. In the South, hundreds of private schools originated to escape integration and were supported at first by state tuition grants (later ruled unconstitutional). "School choice," in short, might very well finance greater racial separation—the choice of whites to stick with their own kind—and at public expense.

The Right's assault on environmental regulation has a similar profile. Taking the lead are small landowners or Western farmers who make appealing pleas to be left alone to enjoy their property and take care of it conscientiously. Riding alongside are developers and major industrial sectors (and polluters) eager to win the same rights, if not from Congress then the Supreme Court. But there's one problem: The overwhelming majority of Americans want stronger environmental standards and more vigorous enforcement.

V. ARE THEY RIGHT ABOUT AMERICA?

"Leave me alone" is an appealing slogan, but the Right regularly violates its own guiding principle. The antiabortion folks intend to use government power to force their own moral values on the private lives of others. Free-market right-wingers fall silent when Bush and Congress intrude to bail out airlines, insurance companies, banks—whatever sector finds itself in desperate need. The hard-right conservatives are downright enthusiastic when the Supreme Court and Bush's Justice Department hack away at our civil liberties. The "school choice" movement seeks not smaller government but a vast expansion of taxpayer obligations. Maybe what the Right is really seeking is not so much to be left alone by government but to use government to reorganize society in its own right-wing image. All in all, the Right's agenda promises a reordering that will drive the country toward greater separation and segmentation of its many social elements—higher walls and more distance for those who wish to protect themselves from messy diversity. The trend of social disintegration, including the slow breakup of the broad middle class, has been under way for several decades—fissures generated by growing inequalities of status and well-being. The Right proposes to legitimize and encourage these deep social changes in the name of greater autonomy. Dismantle the common assets of society, give people back their tax money, and let everyone fend for himself.

Is this the country Americans want for their grandchildren or great-grandchildren? If one puts aside Republican nostalgia for McKinley's gaslight era, it was actually a dark and troubled time for many Americans and society as a whole, riven as it was by harsh economic conflict and social neglect of everyday brutalities.

Autonomy can be lonely and chilly, as millions of Americans have learned in recent years when the company canceled their pensions or the stock market swallowed their savings or industrial interests destroyed their surroundings. For most Americans, there is no redress without common action, collective efforts based on mutual trust, and shared responsibilities. In other words, I do not believe that most Americans want what the Right wants. But I also think many cannot see the choices clearly or grasp the long-term implications for the country.

This is a failure of left-liberal politics. Constructing an effective response requires a politics that goes right at the ideology, translates the meaning of Bush's governing agenda, lays out the implications for society and argues unabashedly for a more positive, inclusive, forward-looking vision. No need for scaremongering attacks; stick to the well-known facts. Pose some big questions: Do Americans want to get rid of the income tax altogether and its long-standing premise that the affluent should pay higher rates than the humble? For that matter, do Americans think capital incomes should be excused completely from taxation while labor incomes are taxed more heavily, perhaps through a stiff national sales tax? Do people want to give up on the concept of the "common school"—one of America's distinctive achievements? Should property rights be given precedence over human rights or society's need to protect nature? The recent battles over Social Security privatization are instructive: When the labor Left mounted a serious ideological rebuttal, well documented in fact and reason, Republicans scurried away from the issue (though they will doubtless try again).

To make this case convincing, however, the opposition must first have a coherent vision of its own. The Democratic Party, alas, is accustomed to playing defense and has become wary of "the vision thing," as Dubya's father called it. Most elected Democrats, I think, now see their role as managerial rather than big reform, and fear that even talking about ideology will stick them with the Right's demon label: "liberal." If a new understanding of progressive purpose does get formed, one that connects to social reality and describes a more promising future, the vision will not originate in Washington but among those who see realities up close and are struggling now to change things on the ground. We are a very wealthy (and brutally powerful) nation, so why do people experience so much stress and confinement in their lives, a sense of loss and failure? The answers, I suggest, will lead to a new formulation of what progressives want.

The first place to inquire is not the failures of government but the malformed power relationships of American capitalism—the terms of employment that reduce many workers to powerless digits, the closely held decisions of finance capital that shape our society, the waste and destruction embedded in our system of mass consumption and production. The goal is, like the Right's, to create greater self-fulfillment but as broadly as possible. Self-reliance and individualism can be made meaningful for all only by first reviving the power of collective action.

My own conviction is that a lot of Americans are ready to

take up these questions and many others. Some are actually old questions—issues of power that were not resolved in the great reform eras of the past. They await a new generation bold enough to ask if our prosperous society is really as free and satisfied as it claims to be. When conscientious people find ideas and remedies that resonate with the real experiences of Americans, then they will have their vision, and perhaps the true answer to the right wing.

Chapter 2
Shrubbed:
The Radical Project of George Bush

―――――――――――

As part of its agenda, the Bush administration has launched a relentless assault on advances made by liberal movements over the last decades—women's rights, civil rights, the environment. The administration even seems intent on challenging the New Deal's judicial revolution, and using the courts to curtail the capacity of Congress to protect consumers, workers, or citizens and hold corporations accountable. The Take Back America conference featured presentations on elements of this agenda, excerpted below.

THE WAR AGAINST WOMEN
by Kim Gandy

THE NEW YORK TIMES called it "The War Against Women." And it *is* a war, a war of attrition. A new abortion procedures ban. Cuts in family planning, both internationally and domestically. The global gag rule that is literally killing women in other countries. It's a war of deception and trickery and lies. Look at Bush and his allies. They've got a bill up there that they describe as a Family Flexibility bill that will let people spend more time with their families. In reality, it has nothing to do with family flexibility; it simply

THE WOMEN'S HOMELAND
TERROR ALERT SYSTEM

SEVERE
PRESIDENT CLAIMS WOMEN DO HAVE RIGHTS:
CAN JOIN ARMY, FIGHT UNPOPULAR WAR,
KILL INNOCENT PEOPLE.

HIGH
PRESIDENT REFUSES TO SIGN INTL. TREATY
ON DISCRIMINATION AGAINST WOMEN.

ELEVATED
PRESIDENT NOMINATES JUDGES OPPOSED TO
AFFIRMATIVE ACTION AND ABORTION RIGHTS.

GUARDED
PRESIDENT APPOINTS MAN TO FDA
WHO BELIEVES PRAYER
IS BEST TREATMENT FOR PMS.

LOW
PRESIDENT RIDES AROUND ON HORSE
CLEARS BRUSH ON RANCH.

www.guerrillagirls.com

Copyright © 2003 by Guerrilla Girls, Inc.

lets companies eliminate overtime pay for millions of workers.

It's a war on many fronts. Now we see the kind of people George W. Bush is nominating to the Federal bench. Judges who violate their oath of office to help cross burners. Judges who say publicly that they believe women should submit to their husbands. Judges who say publicly that violence against women isn't really a serious problem. Judges who say that they would, given the chance, overturn *Roe v. Wade* (which guarantees women's control over their bodies in decisions about reproduction). But it doesn't stop there! The administration is going after Title IX and equal educational opportunity. We all know about the threat to Affirmative Action; they've already gone after the Americans with Disabilities Act, the Age Discrimination Act, the FCC giveaway. . . .

And they call us a "Special Interest." Don't you love it? Women—52 percent of the population—we are a special interest! Halliburton is not a special interest, but women are, people of color are. They're saying, "Oh well, we don't need to hear what you have to say because you're just a special interest. You're not a real person." Then they bring in the corporate types to get their opinions and the real special interests are lining up and filling their pockets. Look at Bechtel, look at Halliburton, all these no-bid contracts. With their connections to Cheney and Bush, it gives new meaning to the phrase "insider trading." Martha Stewart is nowhere in their league. She's down at the tee-ball level; these guys are the pros. But guess who's going to jail? It's not Kenneth Lay of Enron.

Look at WorldCom. Not only is nobody going to jail, they just got one of the biggest contracts in Iraq to rebuild the telephone system! And the biggest special interest in all of this is the media itself—soon to be owned by a handful of Rupert Murdoch cronies that stifle our messages and keep our voices from being heard. . . .

Speaking of Clear Channel, could we hear one round of applause for the Dixie Chicks? How many of you bought your first Dixie Chicks CD after Clear Channel banned them? They have lots of new fans all over the country. All this fuss over their embarrassment at being from Texas—every Texan should be embarrassed . . . their state legislature just played doctor. They not only set a 24-hour waiting period for a woman who is seeking an abortion (like she hadn't thought about it for 24 hours). They also required that before she can have an abortion, the doctor has to tell her that abortions cause breast cancer. Never mind that it's not even true! The doctor has to tell a patient lies to be allowed to perform an abortion in Texas. . . .

I am unapologetically liberal . . . I'm proud to be left, but I'm tired of being left out! I'm tired of being called a "splinter group," but you know, sometimes you just have to take back the language. We're all of us "splinter groups." We're about to get ourselves together and become a two-by-four! I'm tired of people who call themselves leaders whose idea of leadership is to say, "Which way were they going? How many were there? What were they saying? I have to find them, I'm their leader!" Their idea of leadership is putting your finger up to see which way the wind goes and going that way.

But we have a great legacy here. I was so privileged last year to share this platform with the late Senator Paul Wellstone. The loss of Paul and Sheila Wellstone weighs heavily on all of us. A couple of weeks ago we had a meeting where there were over a dozen very progressive senators in the room. One of the things that I took that opportunity to do was to ask each of them to take a little time to stand in Paul Wellstone's shoes. Whether it was a month, a week, a day, an hour . . . , a minute on the Senate floor, to do what Paul Wellstone would have done. . . . We can all do it. We can speak the truth without apology. We can take a stand and we can lead by example. Everyone in this room can do that and I ask you to think on a regular basis, "What would Paul Wellstone do? And what can I do to continue the Wellstone legacy?"

If we're going to turn all those splinters into a two-by-four, we're going to have to change our lives for the next months. And I really mean that in a very serious way. . . . Every single day we need to think, "What must I be doing today so that the outcome of the 2004 election takes back this country for the people it belongs to, not for the special interests? What can I do?" For some of you, it may mean giving up a vacation and spending those two weeks in a state where your help is needed. For some of you, it may mean changing your plans, not doing something you do every Monday night and going to work in a phone bank instead. . . . It can be something big, like quitting your job and going to Iowa. Or something small, like giving up your tall double-latte frappachino and giving that $3.50 to a campaign that's going to make a difference.

I want to ask every one of you . . . to think about what you can do to change your life, to change your direction, to make a difference in the next few months. We have all got to work like our future depends on it, because it does.

•   •   •

ROLLING BACK BASIC RIGHTS
by Wade Henderson

CIVIL RIGHTS ISSUES ARE too often considered issues of the past. But civil rights are right now concerns. The fight to preserve the integrity of the federal courts . . . Making certain that there is an education system that, in fact, does provide equal opportunity for every American child . . . Protecting the right to vote in a fundamental way. We can never have another election like we had in 2000. Civil rights are about making sure that every American is treated fairly. So if we guarantee the right to work based on the fact that people should be evaluated based on their performance on the job, not by their skin color or their agenda, then we have to also guarantee the right to work for gays and lesbians and people whose sexual orientation may be different than the majority. That's what civil rights are about, and that's what we fight for.

We stand for two propositions. One, in coalition there is strength. . . . We have the greatest, most diverse representative democracy. If you are not forging political unity, you can't expect to win. Secondly, you have to have an aggressive affirmative agenda. Playing defense is not enough. You have to be able to focus on the future. You've got to be able to offer something positive as an alternative to the negative messages that bombard us every day. . . .

I believe in the power of bipartisanship. Yes, Democrats have been the catalysts for social change over the last forty years. But every civil rights bill that's been enacted in this country has required not only Democratic votes, but also the votes of moderate Republicans. And unless you are able to forge a unity around these important issues, you can't advance your affirmative agenda. You can play defense, but you can't advance your affirmative agenda. . . .

But now, something fundamentally different is happening in the country. Ideological extremism on the right makes achieving bipartisanship more difficult than ever before. . . . You can't have bipartisanship when one side is playing hardball and the other side is playing softball. . . . You can't have bipartisanship when one side treats you like a tornado treats a trailer park and on the other hand, asks you to disarm unilaterally. . . . You can't have bipartisanship when a leading thinker on the Right, Grover Norquist, says, "bipartisanship is like date rape." Bipartisanship can only be achieved when you know that you can fight back and prevent the other side that has an ideologically driven agenda from rolling back everything you stand for.

Recently the Leadership Conference on Civil Rights published a report entitled, "The Bush Administration Takes Aim: Civil Rights Under Attack." You can pick it up off of our Website [www.civilrights.org]. It exposes not only what are the overt actions, but also what is happening just beneath the surface that most Americans never see, but that affects us in very direct ways.

The assault of the Bush administration has led the civil rights community into a series of pitched battles. First is to stop the packing of the courts. The real question is not just who sits on these courts. The real threat we face is an ideological agenda to enforce new doctrines based on principles of states' rights that will cut back on the ability of Congress to remedy discrimination. When courts start making 5–4 decisions that cut back on the Americans with Disabilities Act or the Violence Against Women Act or erode the Civil Rights Act of '64, they are pushing an ideological agenda that will undermine the rights of all of us. That's why stopping the packing of the courts is so important.

Second, we fought the Bush Administration tax cuts not because we are experts in tax policy, but because we know that driving up the deficits is used to limit the ability of government to respond to the problems of ordinary people. If you don't have the money in the federal budget, how do you prohibit discrimination? How do you protect the environment? How do you stand up on behalf of women? That's why the tax cuts became such a high policy issue.

Third, we're responding to the war that the Bush administration has declared on the American worker and labor unions. When they attacked ergonomic regulations and scorned them as junk science, did they ever talk to the women and men who shuck oysters on the Eastern shore or who pluck chickens? Or did they even look at their fingers, fingers gnawed by rheumatoid arthritis because of repetitive stress injuries? When the administration uses regulations to undermine Title IX of the education amendments of '72 that protect women and girls in schools and in institutions of higher education, we can't let them pass under the radar. Title IX has been central to lifting the glass ceiling on women. The fact that you have so many women here today as progressive activists, as the head of national organizations standing up on equal footing with men and demanding progressive change is in large measure because of Title IX.

The administration also uses litigation to rollback rights, as demonstrated by the University of Michigan affirmative action case brought to try to gut civil rights laws. Affirmative action, they argue, isn't needed. If you are worried about inequality, the administration says, focus on primary education. But then the president breaks his own promise to fund the No Child Left Behind Act by some $8 billion, while giving every millionaire a massive tax break. And then he had the gall to call himself the education president. That's nonsense. . . .

● ● ●

TRASHING THE ENVIRONMENT
by Deb Callahan

EACH OF US HERE today has a unique perspective about what we want to take back here in America. First I want to talk about what the League of Conservation Voters—what environmentalists across this country—believe that we have to take back. . . .

We hope this year to command a green army of environmentalists and conservationists across this country, mobilized in a way that you've never seen. . . . We intend to take back the environment from the corporate interests and give the environment back to the people because we know that the environment is a precious thing that we need to protect for future generations. I want to give you a better sense of just why this imperative is so important, what we've seen in this Bush administration. . . .

Later this month the League of Conservation Voters is going to release our annual presidential report card on the environment. . . . I can't exactly blow the lid here and tell you what the grades the president is going to get, but I can tell you that last year President Bush and his administration got a D- on the report card.*

* Editor's note: When the League's report card did come out, the president and his administration received the failing grade of F.

This is undeniably the worst administration that we have seen in the history of this nation on these issues. And it's time to tell the truth! . . .

People care about the quality of our air. People care about the cleanliness of our water. People care if they live in communities that are contaminated by toxic waste that's just lying there by a kid's playground.

So let me tell you what this administration has done on these three issues. They have a "Clear Skies" initiative. They say it would achieve limited reductions in sulfur oxides, nitrogen oxides, and mercury in the air. Their plan actually would repeal and weaken current public health protections of the current clean air act—and allow more pollution, causing more asthma and agony. The new Source Review is also another law undermining clean air. The Bush administration would weaken the provision of the Clean Air Act that says, when you build a new power plant, you have to make sure you build a cleaner power plant. You need to make sure you continue not to put more pollution in the air. So basically we're looking at a rollback of the Clean Air Act.

Clean water. . . . The president has reneged on his pledge of no net loss of wetlands; he has also bowed to real estate development interests to limit the scope of the Clean Water Act. In effect, about 60 percent of rivers, lakes, and streams would not be protected under this administration's idea of what a Clean Water Act should look like.

Finally, on toxics. President Bush has failed to support the Polluter Pays Tax. He doesn't think that polluters should clean up their pollution. He doesn't think that people who cared so little as to dump toxic waste into their communities are the people who should clean up the toxic waste. He wants to give the bill to taxpayers rather than the corporations who put those toxics into the ground. . . . A common and disturbing theme pervades these rollbacks and repeals: each was supported by powerful industries that had much to gain. . . .

The question now is will he get away with this? There's something you may not know. There are about 10 million members of environmental groups around this country, 10 to 11 million members who wrote a check and joined an environmental organization. Over 70 percent of the public self-identifies as environmentalist. There are about 12 million members of labor unions in this country today. Do you begin to think of the environmental community as being nearly as politically powerful as labor in this country? You probably don't. And why is that? It's because environmentalists don't think of ourselves as being politically organized that way. And we aren't organized that way. That's the challenge.

There's a sleeping giant out there that's called the national environmental and conservation community, and our job over the next seventeen months is to awaken that sleeping giant. Over the next election, the League of Conservation Voters, the Sierra Club, and environmentalists around this country are going to make sure that we rally our troops in a way that you have never seen before. . . .

One last thought I want to leave you with. One of the most amazing experiences of my life was a dinner where I sat next to Stuart Udall, former Secretary of Interior back in the '60s, who was a spectacular man. And I said, "What was it like? What was it like when you were running the Interior Department and you all created the Endangered Species

Act? You protected amazing lands; you did these new and insightful and far reaching things to protect our natural environment? What was it like to be working in government in those days?" And he said, "Well, you know, basically if you could think it up, you could do it." I couldn't even imagine! I've come to realize that's my guiding principle here. I want to return to a time in this country when if we can think it up, we can do it. And so with that, dream, work, win together!

•   •   •

"PACKING THE COURTS"
by Ralph G. Neas

THIS IS THE MOST Right-wing administration in modern American history. George W. Bush, Karl Rove, John Ashcroft, Dick Cheney—you know the team—are promoting a two-pronged strategy. The first prong is reckless, massive tax cuts. This is not about devising a wise tax strategy. It is a concerted, premeditated effort to take away the money from the federal government over the next couple decades—six trillion dollars' worth. What do they want to do? George Bush's unofficial field marshal Grover Norquist put it well—he said his goal is to shrink the federal government in half so that it's small enough to drown in the bathtub. Now there's a vivid vision for American social policy.

This is a fight over the role of the government. The Far Right doesn't want us to have the money to . . . invest in public health care, public education, or make sure that Medicare and Social Security are solvent for the rest of our nation's history.

© 2002 by Ann Telnaes.
Used with permission.
All rights reserved.

The second part of the strategy is to pack the federal courts. Take away the money, and take away the rights. That is the strategy of the Bush administration and its allies. . . .

George W. Bush has said that he will nominate justices in the mold of Clarence Thomas and Anthony Scalia. If . . . he puts just one or two more right-wing justices on the Supreme Court, they could overturn more than 100 Supreme Court precedents—*Roe v. Wade*, yes, but also environmental protections, civil rights protections, and religious liberty. They want to remove the constitutional basis for much of our social safety net by reinterpreting the commerce clause, the spending clause, and the fourteenth amendment, so that we can't address health care, we can't address public education and save Social Security and Medicare. That's what this is all about—removing the constitutional basis for a progressive government. . . .

We're going to fight back. We're going to have an army and we're going to have a message. This is not going to be about process or about filibusters. It's going to be about what's at stake, for every American—what taking away these seventy years of precedents would do to the daily lives of every American, their children, and their grandchildren. . . .

We have to say, "We're not going to take it anymore." George W. Bush, Tom DeLay, Bill Frist, Trent Lott, Ashcroft, they are the schoolyard bullies and what do we do with schoolyard bullies? We stand up to them! We stand up to them and fight. Filibuster, if necessary. But we just don't take it lying down. . . .

I am optimistic about the next five months, the next seventeen months, the next decade or two, because we're going to convince people that we have to preserve our constitutional rights and freedom. We have to preserve economic justice and extend it. We have to make sure that we convey to America that everything that we've achieved in these last sixty-five years, everything we believe in, everything that we've fought for, is in serious jeopardy.

Paul Wellstone, shortly before he died, put it very well. "The future of America belongs to those who have passion and those who are willing to make the personal commitment to make things better in this country." Those in this room, those listening in the audience, throughout this country today, you have the passion, you have the personal commitment. Together we are going to build an even better America.

Progressive Alternatives: An Economy That Works for Working People

CHAPTER 3
The Progressive Jobs and Growth Agenda

We challenge the reactionary agenda of this administration. But progressives must do more than that. We must lay out clearly a compelling agenda that takes on that of the movement conservatives, the new imperialists and the oil barons now in power. Here, the economist James K. Galbraith lays out the critical elements of that agenda.

FULL ECONOMIC RECOVERY AND FULL EMPLOYMENT
by James K. Galbraith

YOU'VE SUNG THE HYMNS and heard the readings. This is the sermon. To begin on a somber note, the bubble and the bust of high technology, the debt build-up of American households, the obsession with a strong dollar—all of this existed before we got George Bush. The late 1990s were a fine time, but they set the stage for a slump which began in late 2000, from which we have not recovered, and will not recover in full for a long time.

Today almost nine million are unemployed. Many millions more are underemployed, and most of all, underpaid. That

* This piece is adapted from a larger version that will appear in The New Democracy Project's anthology, *What We Stand For: A Progressive Platform for a Changing America.*

is our economic problem. Bush and company did not entirely create these conditions, but they have done nothing to make them better and much to make them worse. We have lost well over two million jobs since he took office, and we have failed to create many millions more that we need.

Full economic recovery is going to be hard. It is not only a matter of spending more. Excess capacity affects the future of business investment no matter what. The reputation of American financial markets has been damaged by fraud and abuse. American households know they are in financial trouble. So far, they are spending every extra dollar—but for how long? If interest rates rise, as is very possible after the election, household spending will be hit hard. And meanwhile quite a bit of what households do spend, with extra income, drains away to imports.

In the near term, new tax cuts and more military spending are bringing another false dawn. The Republicans know when the election will be held. Alan Greenspan—does anyone remember him?—will do his best to keep the housing bubble blown up. Mr. Greenspan knows about blowing bubbles, but not even he can forever prevent them from popping. These measures may work for a time but they will not bring us back to full employment.

The men in charge talk about growth, but actually they won't push growth further than politics requires. Do they really want full employment and strong labor unions and rising wages? I doubt it. Stagnation helps to justify more tax cuts. Their goal is plain: that financial wealth should be freed of tax. First, estate and income taxes were cut. The next year it was capital gains, dividends, and again the top tax rate. Next, the sunset provisions in these measures will be removed. Quite soon, taxes will fall mainly on real estate, payrolls, and current consumption. Which is to say, taxes will be paid mostly by the middle class, by the working class, and by the poor.

As financial wealth escapes tax, neither states nor cities nor the federal government can provide vital services—except by taxing sales and property at rates that will provoke tax rebellions. Every public service will fall between the hammer of tax cuts and the anvil of deficits in state, local, and federal budgets. The streets will be dirtier; so will the air and the water.

Emergency rooms will back up even more than they have; more doctors will refuse public patients. More firehouses and swimming pools and libraries will be closed. Public universities will cost more; . . . Public schools will lose the middle class. Eventually federal budget deficits will collide with Social Security and Medicare, putting privatization back on the agenda. I am from Texas, where you can see this future happening now.

We need to talk about the world outside. To the men in charge, it appears that the world outside is not really a partner or an ally. It is mainly a supplier of cheap labor and cheap oil. I want to stop short of saying that we went to Iraq for the oil. We don't know that. But we do know that when we got there, we found that the oil was there, and the weapons of mass destruction were not.

The fact is we are acquiring an empire. But the men in charge do not want to pay for it. They have no serious interest in providing security, infrastructure or civil administration to the territories they have conquered. And indeed none of these things is being provided. Yet the burdens of empire can only grow as time passes. Sooner or later, we will have to choose between leaving our conquered territories or putting in the full force required to control them. One way we lose control, while the other can only add to the miseries of our balance of payments. How can the cost be met, especially, if the coin of our realm, the U.S. dollar, is at the same time losing its position? It won't be easy. The problem of empires, historically, is not military defeat. It is bankruptcy. Empires do not tend to business at home, and they tend to lose out to rivals who do. As once with Britain and America, so now with America and Europe? That could be how it will turn out. Do we want this? Much as we may admire and like our European friends, I don't think we do.

There is irony here for America's wealthy. While Bush may leave them untaxed, he will not leave them rich as they were. Already their stocks are off by trillions. Soon it may be their houses (and ours). And finally, as the dollar declines, it will be their cash holdings. *An economy that fails for working Americans cannot work, in the long run, for the wealthy.*

What then is our alternative? This is not a moment for "me-too" politics. If you accept the Bush administration's agenda on taxes, or on empire, the game is up. You can't escape from the rest. This is a moment for serious alternatives or none at all.

An economy that fails for working Americans cannot work, in the long run, for the wealthy. Let us therefore reject the vision of America as the New Rome. Collective security made possible the modern world. Only collective security can maintain it. It is the only security solution that is cheap enough to afford, and solid enough to endure. It is the only kind of security there really is.

Our military knows this. They can win any given battle. But can they provide the secure and stable environment afterward? Of course not. Fantasies of missile defense, of more preventive wars, of small nuclear weapons all presuppose a power and intelligence we do not actually have. In practice, in reality, empire is mainly a matter of garrisons. But how many young Americans do we really want to commit, on a permanent basis, to duty in places where they will be shot at and bombed, day after day, until finally we say, "enough?"

We need a new vision of who we are in the world. Let it rest on building up our friends and neighbors. Let us again be committed to building the core capacities—in education, public health, housing, transport—that underpin real development and also our own exports. We need, in the end, to pay our way in the world as honest countries do, and as we used to, mainly with the products of our labor and our knowledge. This means in particular that we must affirm the priority of national interest over that of the renegade corporation. No more Enrons—that global symbol of the corruption of our presence in the wider world.

At home, let us pursue the old goal of full employment—now using our public capacities as needed, until the private sector is ready to resume the lead. As Keynes said, "There is work to do." There are people to do it. Let us bring them together. If interest rates are low, why shouldn't states and localities borrow—with a federal guarantee—and do the work that needs to be done? The principle is simple: Public activity should grow—not contract—when people and resources are unemployed.

We need many creative and productive private enterprises; they should be part of our coalition. But let us also build on the solid and mostly public foundations of education, health, safety, and a clean environment. Let us invest in our science and technology.

We need utilities like water, power, and basic communications under effective public regulation or in public hands. Let us also diversify our energy sources, begin the conserving transformation of our cities and transportation networks, and reduce—prudently—our dependence on oil. And Social Security and Medicare are the pillars of life in this country for the elderly. They must be defended and protected for as long as it takes. The elderly are not going to go away; the only real question is whether we provide and care for them properly or not.

Moving forward, we must finally design a decent system of health care for all. We must raise the minimum wage. We must support collective bargaining and restore a legal climate within which unions can work. We can fight poverty by protecting and expanding the Earned Income Tax Credit. And to protect those in deepest trouble, let's keep personal bankruptcy safe and legal. . . .

To meet the state and local fiscal crisis with a concrete proposal, let me return to what was once a Republican idea. Revenue sharing can prevent the worst cuts in schools and firehouses and basic health services over the next few years. We should make this a flagship program, on a scale large enough—say 50 billion dollars a year for three years—to make a serious difference. I'd propose twice that if I thought it was realistic. The point is that states and localities should not be cutting services at all. And only federal help can prevent what is socially and economically destructive.

To pay for this, not immediately but over the years ahead, the Bush tax cuts should be repealed as needed to pay for what we need to do—especially those elements that serve to reward the misanthropic rich. To our friends among the wealthy of this country, let us say plainly: You are better off being prosperous and paying tax, than going down in the first-class cabins of a sinking ship.

Our task is not merely to boost the economy for a year or two. Even Republicans can do that. Our task is to prepare for a different and better world. It is to build an economy that really does work for working people.

And for that, we need to be serious about what we think, what we say and what we propose. The times call for substantial departures. They will require that we redefine and restate what we stand for in the country. They will require that we reaffirm what our country ought to stand for in the world. We can begin that task here today.

Chapter 4
Top Down or Bottom Up: America's Fateful Choice

═══════════════

Against the "trickle-down economics" of the Right, former Labor Secretary Robert B. Reich suggests a "people-first economics." The latter is better policy and better politics, too.

A Program for a New Majority
by Robert B. Reich

Not to be disrespectful to our current president, but it's still the economy, stupid. Yes, of course, jobs are beginning to return as the economy strengthens. It would be a minor miracle if, given a prime interest rate at 1 percent, the economy didn't strengthen. But even so, by Election Day 2004, there will still be fewer jobs in the United States than there were at the start of this administration.

This is quite an achievement. Not since Herbert Hoover was in the White House has America actually lost jobs during a single term of an administration. George W. Bush does not deserve the entire blame, just as Bill Clinton doesn't deserve all the credit for the 22 million new jobs created on his watch, or the 10 million created during his first term. I was Secretary of Labor during that time, and I deserve the credit. To be serious, a president has one very important lever at his disposal—fiscal policy. Bill Clinton used that lever responsibly. George W. Bush has not.

The Bush administration's fiscal policy is deeply flawed. At a time in our nation's history when the gap between rich and poor is wider than the Gilded Age of the 1890s, and every rung on the income ladder is wider apart than it's been in more than a century, giving a giant tax break to people at the top is socially and morally shameful. It's also economically senseless.

People who are very rich are not going to turn around and spend the extra money. The very definition of being rich is you already spend as much as you want to spend. Those who are most likely to spend the extra money they get from a tax rebate are people of modest means, and yet a comparatively small proportion of the Bush tax break goes to the middle class and an even smaller proportion goes to people in the bottom 20 percent of incomes.

The White House and its radical-conservative allies say that the average American will get back $1,000. But when you hear this administration talk about "averages," watch your wallets. Shaquille O'Neal and I have an "average" height of six feet two inches. An "average" doesn't tell you anything when the big guys are doing so well. The "average" American may get $1,000, but that's because most people get back a few hundred dollars and millionaires get back over $90,000.

The tax cut is so large that some new spending will occur, and thus the economy will get a slight burst of energy. But this is an extraordinarily inefficient way to stimulate the economy. Bush's tax cuts will generate a huge structural deficit for years to come, and they will only increase the deep problem of widening inequality.

It would be far better to give the tax cut to average working people—perhaps in the form of a payroll tax holiday on the first 15 to 20 thousand dollars of their income. A majority of Americans pay more in payroll taxes than they do in income taxes. Hence, this sort of cut would put extra money directly into their pockets, and do so almost immediately. Temporary losses to the Social Security trust fund could be made up simply by removing the cap from the payroll tax and requiring those earning over $88,000 to contribute payroll taxes on their full earnings.

Another worthy strategy for stimulating the economy would be to help the states, which are now some $80 billion dollars in the hole. Almost every state is barred by its state constitution from engaging in deficit spending, and they dare not raise taxes. As a result, the states are in the process of making drastic cuts in spending on education, Medicaid, and social services. Most of these cuts are falling heavily on the middle class and the poor. Many of our most vulnerable citizens being double hurt—but these state cuts and by federal cuts in low-income housing, job training, and related social services. These state cuts also amount to a fiscal drag on the nation's economic recovery.

The Bush tax cuts were never really intended to stimulate the economy in any event. Their purpose was to reward the administration's wealthy friends, and at the same time to starve the government so that there's no money left for Social Security, Medicare, education, health care, or anything else. Privatization of such services becomes a more palatable alternative when there's no money for public provision.

The administration has offered another justification for the tax cuts. They say their purpose is to spur long-term economic growth. We have been here before. Republicans tried supply-side trickle-down economics in the Reagan administration. They ended up with a giant deficit, and nothing trickled down. Trickle-down economics is really trickle *on* economics. When the Clinton administration came to office in 1993, we had to wield a giant pooper-scooper to clean up the mess of twelve years of Republican economics. Now they are at it again.

If wealthy people have more money to invest, they're not necessarily going to invest it in the United States. In case you hadn't noticed, we are in a global economy. The extra money of the rich is going to trickle out, wherever in the world it can summon the highest return. Supply-side economics does not build up America.

How do you build up the American economy? How do you build up the productivity over the long term of Americans? You invest in education and health care. You invest in our people's capacity to be productive. That is not trickle-down economics. It is bubble-up economics. By investing in our people—in the one resource that's relatively immobile in this global economy—we give every one of our citizens a direct stake in our prosperity. We widen the circle of prosperity. We build a sustainable American prosperity. This is what Progressives have stood for for more than a century. It is what we should stand for now.

One final thing. Some Washington hands—pollsters,

political counselors, self-styled political soothsayers—say Democrats must move to the center if we want to get back into power. But I ask you: Where is the center? How do you know it when you've found it? The old Washington hands have a simple answer. You find the center by looking at the polls. The problem with this approach is that it makes it impossible for Democrats to lead. You can't lead America if you are leading people to where they already are. Because they're already there.

I do credit Republican conservatives in this one respect. They do not unduly rely on polls. They stick to what they know, and they stick to their values. Those values are wrong, but they stick to them anyway. They stick to them for years. They tell the same big lies over and over. And George Orwell understood the strategic advantage of such a practice. Republicans know that if they stick to their values—even though they're wrongheaded, even though they're bad for the public, even though Republicans have to tell lies in order to convince people their values are in the public interest—eventually people will follow. That's especially true if the public hears no clear and consistent alternative, if the public doesn't know what the other side stands for.

Democrats used to have strong values. They used to be on the side of the little guy, the underdog, the person who worked hard but got a bad deal, the person who was over-looked by the wealthy and powerful in society. Democrats didn't need to resort to big lies because the truth was clear for everyone to see. And it still is.

What the public actually yearns for is people who stick their values and say what they believe and believe what they say. Ask Americans the following question: "Do you believe that people should be paid enough so that they can lift their family out of poverty, if they are working full time?" And an enormous number, 90 percent, say yes. "Do you believe that every American should be given an opportunity through education, to make the most of his or her God-given rights?" Americans overwhelmingly say yes. "Do you believe that there ought to be a higher minimum wage?" and they overwhelmingly say yes.

I remember when the Clinton administration started thinking about supporting a minimum wage campaign. Quite a lot of old Washington hands said we'd never get a minimum wage increase. They assumed most Americans don't want it, because it just affected people at the lowest rungs of the economy. So I suggested to Dick Morris, the president's pollster that he do a survey, find out what people really thought. (It was the only thing I ever asked of Dick Morris.) He came back right away—I believe it was the next morning. I do not know how he did those surveys so quickly. Maybe he surveyed his family. He came back and said, "It's amazing, 85 percent of Americans believe that there should be an increase in the minimum wage, because it is the fair thing to do."

Ask Americans about health care, now when co-payments, deductibles, and premiums are soaring, when employers are shifting more and more of the costs of health care on to their employees. Ask them whether they feel there ought to be universal affordable health care. Overwhelmingly Americans say yes, there should be.

All Democrats have to do is listen. They don't need polls.

The values of Americans are with us and we are with the values of Americans.

Don't get hung up on the polls. Stick to the values. Stand up for what we believe in.

And then, above all, organize, and mobilize, and energize. We've got to convince the people who have given up on politics, that politics is the applied form of democracy. If you give up on politics, you give up on everything; you cede politics and democracy to the other side. We've got to say to people, who are escaping, denying reality, that escapism and denial and resignation and hopelessness are great enemies of genuine progressive change. Organize, mobilize, and energize—stick to our values and our principles, and have the courage of our convictions—and we will win.

Chapter 5
Growth Is Not Enough

In the modern economy, full employment is necessary before wages start going up across the board. But growth alone is not enough, as Barbara Ehrenreich argues, after revealing the world of low wage work at the height of the Clinton economy.

Empowering Working People
by Barbara Ehrenreich

My CONCERN THIS morning is with the 30 percent of the workforce . . . that lives in poverty, working people living in poverty. These are disproportionately women, single mothers often, and people of color. Now the working poor are not a big concern to our leaders. For example, the president has said that welfare reform, which threw four million single moms into the workforce, was "a resounding success." . . . He doesn't say a whole lot about poverty, but when he does it's kind of interesting. Here's a quote . . . from President Bush: "There are pockets of poverty in America which we cannot let them remain, I mean I refuse to allow them to continue on." I actually love a man who can stand up to the English-only movement! You know, just say what you want!

What would the Bush administration do if they decided to do something about poverty anyway? Bomb it? . . .

What I want to talk about briefly is what kind of programs or demands we should put forward in a time of rising unemployment. With high unemployment, those of us on the Left tend to focus on one thing: the need for more jobs—economic growth, job creation. Everything we talk about tends to narrow down to that. . . . The tighter the labor market, presumably the more valuable labor becomes. It gets easier to leave a bad job, and harder for management to replace you, so they think twice about firing you. So wages should rise if there is decreased unemployment. Now, this is true to an extent. Wages did rise in the late '90s, including for the poorest and least-paid workers, up about $1.00 an hour for those who were getting $5.50 an hour in 1996.

But the surprising thing, and this is what I want to emphasize, is how little they rose in the 1990s. That is how poorly the law of supply and demand seemed to work. In 2000, Alan Greenspan was happily reporting that the economic law linking low unemployment to wage increases seemed to have been repealed. Inflation wasn't happening, not from wage increases anyway. This was great news for the business class. But the low unemployment economy of the late '90s was not an economy that works for working people.

When I did research for my book, *Nickel and Dimed*, I went out and worked in different low-wage jobs because that's all I could get, frankly. My background, an ancient Ph.D. in biology, gets you, maybe, onto the floor of Wal-Mart. I worked alongside women who were homeless—full-time working people who were homeless. They didn't consider themselves homeless because in America today we have a hierarchy of homelessness. If you have a vehicle to sleep in, you don't call yourself homeless.

I also worked alongside people who were not getting enough to eat during the workday. . . . And I will admit that my middle-class bias, when I saw women skipping lunch or just eating a little bag of Doritos, was to assume, "Oh, she must be dieting." Was I ever wrong. They didn't have money; they didn't have food. Now this was in the boom years. This was in the best of times when unemployment was only 4 percent.

Why didn't low unemployment work better for working people? Well, I've got some speculations. One is the immobility of so many workers. If the law of supply and demand is going to work, you've got to be able to move to the slightly better paying jobs. But people often literally can't get there. Transportation is a wage issue, too. . . . Also, you lose a week's pay, maybe two weeks' pay, if you change jobs. That's not possible for a lot of people.

Second, the *New York Times* reported in 2000 that employers would do anything to avoid raising wages. Why? Because if you raise wages, people are going to expect to get raises all the time. So what employers often did was to add some teeny, tiny benefit. For example, when I worked at Wal-Mart in Minnesota, once a week, if you could arrange your break at the right time, you could have a free donut. Seven dollars an hour doesn't look so bad if you get a free donut every now and then! Another reason supply and demand doesn't work so well is a lack of information. People don't have the information, often, that they need to make informed choices about jobs. Many companies do not even mention wages or benefits or anything like that until you've actually got your uniform on. They don't want to talk about that. They'll do anything to prevent that subject from coming up. Some bosses even forbid discussion of wages among workers. That's illegal, but they forbid it anyway. In fact, many employers I ran into actually forbade talking among employees. So it's hard to get the information you need. So I would say, for one thing, how about a campaign to publicize dismally low wages? I would like to see billboards showing the starting pay at some of our major corporations along with the CEO pay and all the benefits.

At Wal-Mart, you start at $7 an hour. The CEO makes— if you go with Arianna Huffington's wonderful book, *Pigs at the Trough* (not a book about agriculture)—well over $10 million dollars a year. If you go with *USA Today*'s estimate, with stock options he makes $66 million dollars a year. At $7 an hour, it would have taken me only 5,000 years to make what he makes in one year. In all that time, I'd probably have never gotten a promotion because I'm a woman, anyway. So I would like to see a living wage bill passed in every city and town. I would like to see the minimum wage raised to be a wage you could actually live on. I would like to see it become possible for American workers to organize into unions.

Finally, one last reason why just saying, "more jobs, please give us more jobs" is not a sufficient economic program. It leaves out those people who cannot take a job because they're already working. They are working taking care of children. Taking care of children is a lot harder in poverty than taking care of them in a middle-class suburb. Or they are taking care of the elderly or sick spouses. The tragedy of welfare reform was its complete dismissal of this kind of care-taking, the work that goes on in the home, perhaps because it is women's traditional work. I think we need to honor and respect that, too.

So, yes, we need more jobs, definitely. But we cannot measure our success in terms of the number of jobs, we cannot measure it in terms of productivity, we cannot measure it in terms of the growth of the GDP, and we certainly cannot just measure it in terms of corporate profits. The only true measure of our success in the agenda we want to promote is the ability of America's working people to live with dignity and security when they are employed and even when they're unemployed.

SECTION III

KITCHEN TABLE ISSUES

Chapter 6
Health Care—The Logic of Radical Reform

≡≡≡≡≡

Universal, affordable, comprehensive health care is America's great unfinished agenda. The United States remains the sole industrial nation that does not guarantee health insurance for its citizens. Winning this battle is central to a more decent America and central to any progressive reform agenda. Here, Robert Kuttner outlines the logic and the path to comprehensive reform.

HEALTH CARE: THE LOGIC OF RADICAL REFORM
by Robert Kuttner

MOST AMERICANS SAY THAT they want universal health insurance "that can never be taken away," as Bill Clinton memorably put it. But universal health insurance is off the political radar screen, a victim of the power of the health insurance and drug lobbies, the reluctance of large corporations to support a major increase in government functions (that would actually save them money), the ambivalence of the medical profession, and the caution of most mainstream politicians.

A related problem is budgetary. Although universalizing health coverage under government auspices would deliver a far more efficient use of the health dollar for society as a whole, it would have the fiscal effect of shifting nearly a trillion dollars of financial flows from private to public sector, at a time when that seems inconceivable.

Ours is said to be a highly individualistic society. But history has shown that universal programs of social insurance are immensely popular in America once the democratic system mobilizes public support to break through barriers to their enactment. Social Security is the most expensive, redistributive, and socialistic of our public programs. It is wildly popular, and conservative politicians profess loyalty to it even as they seek to undermine it mainly by stealth. Likewise Medicare, our second most universalistic program and an island of single-payer health insurance. Even with the assaults on its funding and reductions in its coverage, Medicare remains far more efficiently administered than any private insurance program, and is exceptionally popular.

The solidarity that these programs engender is self-reinforcing. There is little doubt that universal and public health insurance, if enacted, would be highly prized by voters. This reality was perceived and explicitly articulated by House Republicans in 1993, when they vowed to resist any version of the Clinton health plan for fear that it would bond a new generation of voters to universal social insurance and to the Democratic Party as its steward.

Today, the system of employer-based health insurance combined with the tender mercies of managed care is a shambles. Expenses are out of control, but the cost-containment pinches in the wrong places. Hospitals are shutting their doors while new for-profit hospitals for special surgery leach money from the rest of the system. Most people lack pharmaceutical coverage. Doctors and patients alike resent the bureaucracy, the cost shifting, the denial of necessary care, the interposition of case reviewers between physician and patient, the skimming of scarce health dollars, the paper-chase, the insecurity of coverage, and the plain misallocation of resources.

Managed care, under private insurance auspices, was billed as the market's answer to reliable health coverage. Today's version of managed care is a far cry from its community-oriented antecedent—nonprofit prepaid group health plans. Those plans, such as Kaiser Permanente, Group Health of Puget Sound, and the Health Insurance Plan of Greater New York, offered a semblance of universal heath insurance within one community. They covered preventive care, they offered far better coordination among a team of clinicians than conventional medicine, and then invested in the long-term health of plan members. They were also "community rated," meaning that everyone paid the same premium, so there was the kind of broad pooling of risk and intergenerational compact that a true national health insurance system provides. Care was "managed" in the sense that there was no financial incentive (or disincentive) to provide clinically unnecessary surgery, and the money saved by using health resources more efficiently could be reprogrammed to better preventive care.

Today's version of managed care under the direction of for-profit HMOs has reversed virtually all of these features and incentives. Managed-care organizations maximize profits by "risk-selecting"—targeting relatively healthy subscribers and avoiding sick ones—or by denying necessary care. Physicians have financial incentives to stint on care, not to maximize the right blend of prevention and acute care. As HMOs have given way to loose networks of approved providers, the promise of close collaboration on cases of the old staff or group model practice has largely evaporated. Moreover, managed care has increased fragmentation and diminished patient choice of doctors. And as frustrated consumers move from one insurance company to another, insurers have little incentive to invest in the long-term wellness of their patients. Managed care is just a euphemism for hammering down costs, while contributing to the inefficiency of the system overall. At least $200 billion of the more than $1.3 trillion spent on health care nationally goes for administrative costs and profits that would not exist under a national health insurance program, even as 85 million Americans have been without insurance at one time or another during a recent four-year period.

Meanwhile, the traditional system of employer-provided insurance is unraveling. This system was an accidental byproduct of wage and price controls during World War II. During the era of strong unions, regulated industries, and stable corporate oligopolies of the postwar boom, most large employers provided good health insurance and most workers spent their careers with one employer.

Today, health insurance costs represent a huge drain on company resources, corporations are shifting costs onto employees as fast as they dare, workers who lose jobs or change employers often lose good health insurance, and smaller businesses and newer giants like Wal-Mart often provide no insurance at all. This shifts more costs onto workers or to the public sector, and causes more people to simply forgo necessary care. According to a recent report, fully 26 percent of workers without health insurance, or their dependents, are employed by large companies with 500 or more employees.

This crisis will only worsen in coming years, as science keeps inventing new treatments and cures, as the population ages, and as the federal deficit driven by the Bush tax cuts deepens. We can get a good picture of the Republican approach to the cost crisis. As part of a package tied to grossly inadequate prescription drug benefits, the Republicans have promoted "competition" in the Medicare program. This approach, sometimes called "premium support," has at times been supported by center-right Democratic politicians such as Sen. John Breaux, and by Democratic policy-intellectuals who are mainly concerned with the Medicare cost crisis.

The proposed new system would retain conventional Medicare, but cap the federal contribution to it. In most versions, seniors would be given a voucher worth a fixed amount of money. They could use that voucher toward the cost of either traditional public Medicare or a private plan. However, the costs of decent coverage, public or private, would soon outstrip the value of the voucher. Private insurance companies would target younger, healthier elderly people, and because their payout costs per subscriber would be lower than conventional Medicare, they would continue to skim off the relatively healthier population. Traditional Medicare, meanwhile, would be stuck with an ever sicker and more expensive set of patients, so it would have to cut back what it covered. The system would rapidly fragment into multiple insurers and two basic tiers. More affluent retired people, who could subsidize the government voucher out of pocket, would get adequate coverage, while others would have to choose between necessary medical care and other necessities such as rent and food. The universalism and solidarity-producing benefits of the current Medicare system would be ruined.

If market-based medicine ever enjoyed a presumptive reputation for greater choice and efficiency, that advantage has evaporated. However, because of what political scientist Walter Dean Burnham calls a "politics of excluded alternatives," too many Democrats are thinking too narrowly. Some Democrats fell into the trap of trading gradual privatization of Medicare for a completely inadequate drug benefit. Other Democrats have settled for very modest incremental increases in coverage, at a time when the whole system is built on sand. Still others have proposed a totally self-defeating auto-insurance model, in which citizens would be required to obtain health insurance, and government would subsidize the poor to purchase stripped-down policies. This approach suffers from all the failures of the proposed voucherization of Medicare, and would leave tens of millions of Americans with coverage in name only. It would also introduce demeaning means-testing, which both creates poverty traps (you lose benefits as your income rises) and frustrates the politics of universalism.

Progressives today face a twin challenge. First, we need to return to center-stage universal health insurance as the more efficient and equitable alternative to the current patchwork.

This requires a massive program of public education about the inferiority of market-driven medicine, compared to a universal, government-sponsored system. While we're at it, we need a better term than "single-payer," which is an insider term that mystifies more than it clarifies. My preference is Medicare for All. We need politicians willing to champion it.

Second, we need to defend fiercely the islands of universalism that exist, such as Medicare, and resist voucherization, privatization, and means testing. Any kind of income or asset testing or any voucherization fragments the constituency for universal social insurance. The better the basic package, the fewer people feel the need to purchase supplemental private insurance. More meager the basic benefits, either in a public program or via vouchers, the more the constituency for social insurance splinters.

Third, we need to think hard about the right and wrong kinds of incrementalism. The French radical Andre Gorz used the phrase, "non-reformist reform" to describe modest reforms that logically led to more fundamental reforms. Some partial increments in health coverage logically pave the way more far-reaching changes. Others merely reinforce the fragmentation and the flaws in the current system.

As noted, a number of moderate and liberal politicians have tried to improve health coverage, incrementally, by "filling in gaps" in those who are covered. The State Children's Health Insurance Program (SCHIP), for example, is intended to provide coverage to children who fall between the cracks and receive coverage neither from their parents' policies nor from Medicaid. But SCHIP illustrates everything wrong with this sort of incrementalism. It has slightly increased coverage, but at the cost of reinforcing fragmentation. In the same year, a child can find herself covered by Medicaid, by a plan provided by a parent's employer, and by a state program reimbursed by federal funds under SCHIP. This approach reinforces the administrative complexity, the paperwork, the lack of continuity of care, and the byzantine impenetrability of the system as experienced by ordinary people.

There are several possible approaches to universal health insurance. The most far-reaching would be for Democrats and progressives to put on the table a Medicare for All program, and to organize around it, building support from doctors frustrated by the current mess, trade unionists, editorial writers, elected officials and candidates, and mass-membership organizations. Rep. Dennis Kucinich did this during his campaign for the Democratic presidential nomination, and Physicians for a National Health Program has been doing heroic work on this front, leading to favorable coverage in leading medical journals including both the *New England Journal of Medicine* and the traditionally more conservative *Journal of the American Medical Association*. Doctors have gotten such a screwing from the present system that they are fast becoming political allies.

The long-term strategy needs to be a coalition of forces that puts nearly everyone on one side—doctors, patients, unions, mass-membership groups, seniors in danger of losing Medicare, corporations that stand to save money from a socialization of costs—and two powerful nemesis groups on the other side: the for-profit health insurance industry and the drug companies. President Clinton, in 1993, made the disastrous strategic mistake of thinking that "managed competition," running universal care through private insurance companies, could co-opt their political support. But the companies understood the threat to their autonomy, power, and profit; they preferred to insure fewer people with higher profits and substantial control rather than face government regulation of their plans and premiums. Their answer was Harry and Louise.

If Clinton had gone to the country in the midterm election of 1994 and waged a populist campaign pitting health care for all against the selfishness and inefficiency of the insurance industry, political history might have been very different. A presidential candidate or president with nerve and vision could restore Medicare for All to mainstream debate and could create such a coalition politics.

Pending that long-term strategy, which forms of incrementalism might help seed the ground?

One big first step is universal health care for children— not SCHIP but extension of public, federal Medicare to all kids. Children are very cheap to insure because most don't get sick. For the cost of a repeal of part of the Bush tax cut, well under $100 billion a year, every new baby could get a Medicare card, and every child under eighteen or under twenty-five could be covered within two years. Politically, this would create a powerful intergenerational alliance. It would reduce health costs for employers (who would cover workers but no longer children of workers). And, as children turned eighteen or twenty-five, it would produce powerful political pressure to allow them to keep their coverage.

A variant would combine Medicare for the young with a Medicare buy-in option for people age fifty-five to sixty-five. These are the people who are disproportionately losing their insurance and finding new coverage astronomically expensive to purchase. One combination strategy would cover all children under 18 in 2005, extend that to people under twenty-five and allow the over-fifty-five buy-in in 2006, and then extend Medicare to people forty-five to fifty-five in 2007, and fill in the remaining group, the twenty-five to thirty-five-year-olds, in 2008.

These initiatives would help seniors learn that the way to make Medicare secure is to extend it to other age groups who are less costly to insure and whose participation broadens the Medicare political constituency. They would also help educate politicians of the broader fact that Medicare for All is the only sure way to reconcile the cost crisis with the crisis of declining coverage, and to yoke the political interests of those without insurance to those fearful of losing good insurance.

A whole other approach would be to build universal health programs state by state. This is attractive in principle. But the current state budget crisis makes it improbable. And states typically fall back on fill-in-the-gaps approaches such as Howard Dean's vaunted Dr. Dynasaur program in Vermont, which is far from a true single-payer program, or on employer mandates, another second-best reform that doesn't logically build toward true universalism.

A predicate to any incremental non-reformist reform agenda would be careful thought about its elements and dynamics. A good start would be to create the broadest possible commission for universal health coverage, with representation of physicians, insurance experts, elected officials, trade unionists, academics, and leaders of mass membership organizations. This commission would be tasked with creating both the blueprint for the program, as well as a political and popular-education strategy for bringing it about.

The history of American social insurance is that good ideas remain available, waiting for rare moments, such as 1933–37, or 1941–45, or 1967–68, in which progressives gain rare working majorities. The next time that rare moment occurs, the worst possible thing would be for progressives to settle for modest, partial reform.

At present, the Right dominates Washington. But this is a teachable moment for progressives. The market-based health insurance system is collapsing, and ordinary people are the victims. Regular Americans understand the need for a breakthrough, and the Right's remedies will only worsen the shift of health burdens onto citizens. Progressives need the political courage to indict the Right for its failure, and the leadership to show that a bold and comprehensive alternative is possible.

BOONDOCKS © 2003 Aaron McGruder. Dist. by UNIVERSAL PRESS SYNDICATE. Reprinted with permission. All rights reserved.

CHAPTER 7
America's Commitment to Education

―――――――

Most Americans believe that every child has the right to a high quality public education. But our current education debate does not begin to address the daunting challenge now facing our teachers. Here Robert L. Borosage and Earl Hadley outline the elements of that challenge which the much advertized Bush agenda does not even begin to address. Rousing this country to make the commitment necessary is surely central to the progressive agenda.

EDUCATING THE NEXT GENERATION: AMERICA'S HISTORIC CHALLENGE
Robert L. Borosage and Earl Hadley

GEORGE BUSH HAS STARTED talking about education again, a sure sign that 2004 is an election year. The President will tout his education reforms as a centerpiece of the "compassionate conservatism" certain to be revived for the election campaign. Bush's poll-packaged Administration understands that schools are a central concern of voters, particularly the now-iconic "soccer moms."

Sadly, the President's posturing is not reflected in his priorities. His No Child Left Behind reform bill imposes the most ambitious federal mandates on the schools since the civil rights reforms of the 1960s. Bush gained bipartisan support for punishing schools that don't measure up on tests by providing parents with the right to transfer to another public school, while promising significant new funding to pay for school improvement. He then reneged on that commitment, failing to budget even the funds he promised, which were already far less than what schools actually needed to meet the mandates. Bush's budget fell $9 billion short of his own promise; he offered Turkey more than that as a bribe to get it to enter the war in Iraq.

Not surprisingly, the emphasis on testing has generated a firestorm of protest. Forced, focused attention on the progress of all students could potentially generate greater commitment to educating the poor and minority students who have been too often dismissed as hopeless. But when the President broke his own commitment on resources to help schools deal with the challenge, he left school districts to struggle with a vastly underfunded mandate. And with states and localities facing the worst fiscal crisis in fifty years, schools—particularly those in poorer neighborhoods—have been forced to cut programs and teachers, not add them. The resulting pressures may reproduce the scandals that marred the Houston schools that were the much-celebrated model for the national reforms. There Bush's Education Secretary Rodney Paige supervised schools that showed progress on tests by routinely increasing and masking dropout rates. Paige made his name in a district that claimed success, while hiding the fact that it was literally leaving children behind.

Yet, even if the President had contributed the funds he had promised for his reforms, he would still have failed the staggering challenge this country faces in educating the next generation of Americans in the new century.

With more than 50 million students and 3 million teachers in 92,000 public schools in 15,000 districts, simply running what has traditionally been a locally governed nonsystem is hard enough. The new information age and the new global economy make education—and lifelong learning—even more essential to our prosperity. A new generation of immigrants requires the schooling vital for assimilation of our language and civic traditions. As communications technologies make the world smaller and generate a growing sophistication in packaging and propaganda, an educated, questioning, independently thinking citizenry is even more vital to our democracy.

Americans understand this. They expect their leaders to make education a priority. They demand ever more from their schools. They are alarmed at reports, often misleading, of their children lagging behind those in other countries in reading, math, or science. Over the past two decades, waves of reform have set higher standards and provided greater resources to schools.

Yet even as public spending on schools has risen over the past two decades, particularly at the state and local level, the national debate about schools has been dominated by a conservative mantra: Money is not the solution, something else is. For the now dominant Republican Right, public schools—where one in four Americans work or study—are an ideological affront. The exodus of whites from the public schools in the South after integration and in urban areas of the North has enabled calculating politicians to turn school funding into a political wedge issue. For two decades, conservatives have scorned public investment in schools, while offering up a menu of alternative "fixes": school prayer, zero tolerance, standardized testing, phonics, English-only immersion, ending certification of teachers, vouchers. They've gone from demanding the abolition of the Department of Education to seeking to supplant the common public school with a "marketplace" of private institutions, all the while opposing increased investment in schools.

For all his photo ops, President Bush reflects this conservative animus. Not only did the President fail to fund his own reform legislation adequately, he also zeroed out funding for new school construction, cut funding for teacher education, failed to extend Head Start to all children eligible, and sought to allow states to siphon funds from the program. And most destructive, the President insisted on his entire package of top-end tax cuts as a "stimulus plan" while opposing targeted aid to prevent layoffs of teachers and cutbacks in school programs that indebted states have been forced to impose. Yet, it is on this record that Bush will undoubtedly campaign in 2004 as an education President.

But the country can no longer afford this default. Consider simply the following:

- This fall, 53 million students will attend elementary and secondary schools in America, the largest number in our nation's history. In the next decade, that number will begin to grow again, ending up at nearly 100 million children in school by the end of the century. A growing number of these students are from immigrant families, newly arrived on our shores speaking little or no English. With one in five children raised in poverty, a significant portion comes to school deprived of the healthy start vital to being ready to learn. One third of all American schoolchildren are needy enough to quality for free or reduced-price school lunches. In New York City, it is 70 percent. In Detroit, 78 percent.

• These students will attend schools that are aged, overcrowded, and underrepaired. America's schools average forty-two years in age, with the oldest often in the areas where the needs are greatest. The influx of students, particularly in urban areas, has led to doubling up classes, half-day shifts, and the conversion of trailers, closets, libraries, and gyms for classrooms. One third of all schools now use trailers to house classrooms. In 1995, the General Accounting Office estimated that it would require $112 billion simply to bring the schools up to safe standards. A more detailed estimate by the National Education Association in 2000 that included funds needed to update schools for advanced technology, estimated the cost at $322 billion.

• These same schools now face the largest wave of teacher retirements ever, as the baby-boom teachers begin to leave the workforce. At the same time, the retention rate of new teachers is shockingly low, with 20 percent of new hires leaving the classroom after three years. One reason is that the starting pay of teachers is among the lowest of all professions requiring a college degree with specialized training. Since 1970, average teacher pay has outpaced inflation by only one third of 1 percent a year. Now women and minorities are no longer locked out of other careers, depriving schools of what had been a captive quality labor pool that could be had on the cheap. Low teacher pay hurts the most in the low-income urban communities that have the greatest need for experienced, skilled, and committed teachers.

• As they graduate, students will seek to enter colleges where tuitions and costs are rising at 14–15 percent a year. Federal grants for deserving students have not kept up with these costs: The maximum Pell grant now covers 39 percent of public school tuition, down from 84 percent in 1975–76. College graduates now leave with debt burdens 35 percent higher than those of students graduating a decade ago. And more and more simply are priced out of four-year colleges altogether. At a time when we ought to be making college education universally available, our commitment is flagging.

There is a legitimate debate about how efficiently money is used in our schools. Too often, when more money is available, sclerotic bureaucratic systems spend it not on meeting specific needs, but on placating entrenched lobbies. Decades of reform fads have come and gone without settling significant disagreements about which reforms make a difference. But beneath the ideological posturing and legitimate debates, there is a common sense agenda for public education.

Children should come to school ready to learn. That means having a healthy start, with good nutrition, health care, and adequate shelter. Preschool is essential in providing basic social, behavioral, and cognitive skills. Children should attend schools that are safe, pleasant to be in, well-equipped, well-lit, and not dangerous to their health. Schools must engage parents, and insure that they are involved and present as much as possible. Small classes make a difference, particularly in early grades when individual attention can give slower starters a needed boost. For working parents, diverse after-school programs are both helpful to children and vital to society. Skilled, experienced, and dedicated teachers are indispensable. They need to be well-prepared and committed to lifelong learning and retraining, and should be rewarded accordingly. Children should know from the start that going on to college is both expected and affordable.

These are neither new nor revolutionary concepts. They don't encompass the latest fad in high-tech education, the latest vogue of small middle schools, or whole child learning. They are the basics. And yet for a dramatic and growing portion of the next generation, they are out of reach.

For that to change, Americans need to hold their public officials accountable. It has been too easy for politicians like George W. Bush to parade as education reformers while refusing to make schools a priority in their budgets, and failing to rally the nation at all levels to make the investments vital to providing the basics for every child.

The politics of this default are poisonous. In 1972, nearly 80 percent of US public school students were white. In 2002, it was barely 60 percent. Imposing underfunded mandates on schools, railing against failing schools, proffering vouchers that weaken the schools further, all the while defaulting on the basic investments needed could easily become a staple in the racial wedge politics that is the foundation of the modern Republican Party. In 2004, the President will boast about his historic reforms, while calling for limits on domestic spending. Yet this is the President who ran up record deficits paying for tax breaks for the already affluent, added $100 billion a year to a military budget that is now nearly as great as the rest of the world's combined, and spent $87 billion to occupy Iraq and Afghanistan for one year alone. At the same time, he claimed we could not afford the funds needed to avoid debilitating cuts in public schools across the country, much less to double the federal commitment to public schools—from 2.8 to 5 percent of the national budget—and lead a renewed commitment at all levels to educating the next generation.

Neither our democracy nor our prosperity can easily withstand this posturing. An educated citizenry has always been a hallmark of America's democracy and a foundation of its progress. That was surely true over the past century, as America rose to global prominence and enjoyed unparalleled prosperity. Education taught a common language and extended a shared civic culture to the flood of immigrants that forged America's industrial might. America became the first country to require twelve years of formal schooling. After World War II with the GI Bill, America became the first nation to make college education widely available. Integrating America's schools was central to the effort to end segregation and address the challenge of equal opportunity for all. This commitment to education helped to forge the broad middle class that is the pride of America's democracy and the foundation of its prosperity.

The workers and the citizens of the next generation will necessarily come in increasing measure from the ranks of today's poor and working-class children. And while the test-score gaps between white and black, and white and Hispanic children have begun to shrink, the gulf between rich and poor achievement in schools remains enormous. If those children are not educated well, and well beyond even the high school level, it is not simply the economy that will suffer, but our democracy itself.

Can we now educate to a high level of achievement a remarkably diverse population of children, drawn from many races and cultures, many with little or no English, many raised in poverty on dangerous streets? No other nation has attempted anything like this. This is the great democratic, economic, and human rights challenge of our time.

To meet this daunting but inescapable mission requires not more posturing, but a renewed commitment to public education. Those who seek to dismantle or starve the public schools should be scorned as the cranks that they are. If we are to provide a high quality public education from pre-school through college to the next generation, we must ante up the resources even as we undertake necessary reforms. That isn't a task for the federal government alone, nor for the states or the localities. It is a task for the nation.

SECTION IV

THE APOLLO INITIATIVE

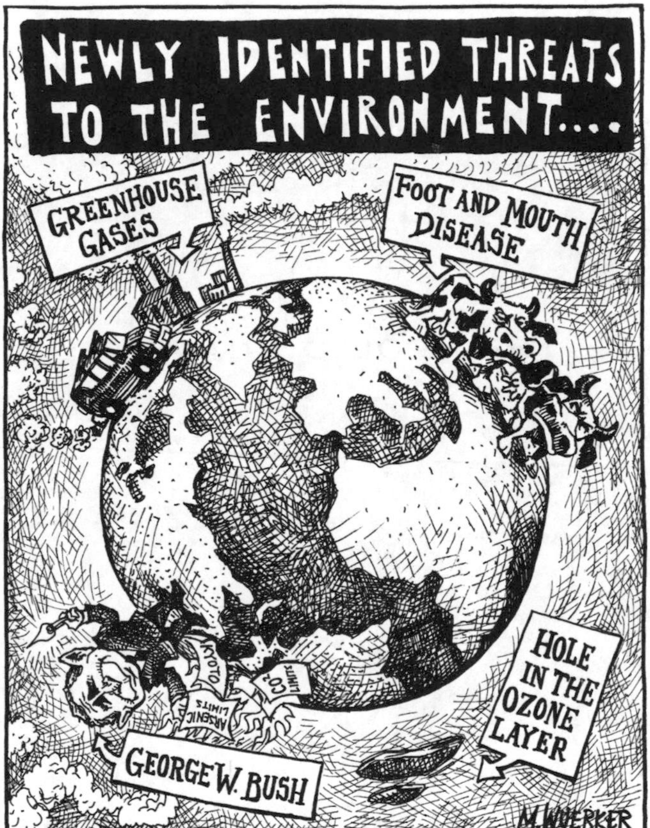

© Matt Wuerker

CHAPTER 8
Jobs and Energy Independence:
The Apollo Initiative

───────

When it comes to the challenges facing Americans, the Bush administration demonstrates that the conservative agenda is, to coin a phrase, part of the problem, not part of the solution. This offers progressives the opening to put forth positive initiatives that address the real challenges facing the country and the American people. These initiatives must be large enough to deal with the problem, broad enough to engage new allies and attract new supporters, clear enough to be both compelling and comprehensible. The Apollo Initiative for Good Jobs Through Energy Independence is an important contribution to a progressive and visionary reform agenda.

THE APOLLO INITIATIVE
by Bracken Hendriks

TOO OFTEN WE ARE told to think small—that we must choose between good jobs and environmental quality, and that we cannot break the crippling dependence on foreign oil that threatens the security of our nation. But we can do better. Working families should not have to choose between putting food on the table for our children today and protecting the health of our children tomorrow. The new Apollo Project seeks to break the zero-sum framework of jobs versus the environment, by putting forward a strategic initiative that works to improve both environmental and economic quality of life. Apollo represents a bold and hopeful vision that unites the progressive base, curbs our addiction to foreign oil, paves the way to a new environmental strategy, and invests in our economic future.

AMERICA'S CHALLENGES

Even at the height of its current power and prosperity, America faces daunting challenges. Our cities and states are experiencing the worst financial crisis since World War II. Programs such as Social Security and Medicare are facing massive budget cuts. Americans are out of work, with this Bush administration managing the worst jobs record of any President since Herbert Hoover and the Great Depression. We're hemorrhaging manufacturing jobs. Our cities face over a trillion dollars of unmet infrastructure needs. This year, millions of Americans faced rolling blackouts. Global warming is a real and growing danger.

The U.S.'s crippling dependence on foreign oil is unsustainable. At the time of the 1973 oil embargo, the United States imported 35 percent of its petroleum. Today we import well over half. The United States consumes a quarter of the world's oil yet has only 3 percent of its reserves, so more drilling offers no solution. Our energy problems go deeper than oil. We use 25 percent of the world's energy, nearly three times the amount of any other country. Deregulation has destabilized the energy sector, contributing to historic blackouts. Further, pollution problems are escalating, and environmental impacts threaten to limit our economic growth and hurt our quality of life.

These big challenges—crises in our environment, in our energy security, in our economy, and in the fabric of our cities—need to be met with big ideas and bold solutions. The Bush administration established a task force under Vice President Cheney to lay out a comprehensive energy policy. But Cheney expressed little but contempt for conservation—a "personal lifestyle," he sniffed—and turned the commission over to the lobbyists from Big Oil and Enron. The result is an energy plan that lards subsidies on energy suppliers, calls for more drilling from Alaska to Florida, and does nothing to reduce our dependence on imported oil. The plan succeeded in sparking a pitched battle, with many labor unions and environmentalists on opposite sides, posing a choice between creating jobs and protecting the environment.

Now moving beyond these false divisions, labor leaders and environmentalists are uniting around a bold new vision for America's future. A new project—of the scope and urgency of the original Apollo Project that took us to the moon decades ago—that would dramatically break our dependence on foreign oil by investing in energy efficient and renewable technology, creating millions of good jobs here at home and building a sustainable infrastructure that will make our communities more livable and more equitable.

THE APOLLO PROJECT: A PATH FORWARD

Named after President Kennedy's famous challenge to put a man on the moon, the new Apollo Project seeks to curb

America's addiction to oil, increase the diversity of our energy resources, invest in new technology, and create new jobs for Americans. Specifically, Apollo calls for a bold $300-billion plan for the next ten years. It will be broad-based, sharing the benefits of investment widely across the economy while insuring that no single sector bears all the costs. And it will be immediate, deploying proven and cost-effective technologies that exist today, not placing all our hopes on long-term R&D like the Bush plan for a hydrogen "freedom car."

Backed by seventeen international labor unions and a broad cross section of the environmental community, the Apollo alliance calls for an investment to jump-start America on the road to energy independence. Investment will accelerate new renewable energy sources. It will convert assembly lines to put American-made advanced technology cars on the road. It will help older plants improve their environmental performance, preserving domestic manufacturing jobs. It will deploy new technology for pollution control at older power plants, and invest in research and development to create a hydrogen energy revolution.

The new Apollo Project will promote high-performance "green" building and push a new generation of energy-efficient appliances to market—driving up efficiency without driving jobs overseas. It will support smart growth and mass transit, increase brownfield redevelopment, and rebuild transportation and water infrastructure, relieving municipal budget pressures. And an Apollo Project will strengthen, not repeal, regulatory protections for consumers, workers, and the environment.

Like Kennedy's Apollo program, the new Apollo Project will put America at the cutting edge of new technology and global economic leadership. At present, America is neglecting the industries of the future while other nations move rapidly to capture them. Wind is the fastest-growing energy source in the world but European producers, not Americans, dominate turbine production. Fuel cells are poised to revolutionize energy technology, but most are produced at nonunion plants in Canada. In 2000, the Japanese government invested more than $500 million to build the market for photovoltaic cells that convert sunlight into electricity, over seven times the U.S. commitment of resources. It is time for America to step up to the plate—to unleash the ingenuity, enthusiasm, and drive that sent a man to the moon.

THE POLITICS OF UNITY

Investing in the Apollo Project means more than dollars and cents; it means investing in a new political strategy. For too long, Democrats have allowed the GOP to exploit old fault lines between economic populists and environmentalists, pitting jobs against the environment and today against tomorrow. But an Apollo Project represents both good policy and good politics.

Voters want a better vision of the future. Recent polls in key Midwestern swing states show strong approval among voters—72 percent support a large-scale Federal program to invest $300 billion on energy independence. Even more striking, support for Apollo jumps to 81 percent among non-college educated, Bush-leaning, Democratic, white men—a segment of the population that often breaks with progressives, and a group that could determine the outcome of the next election. These "Reagan Democrats" have been burned by the current economy, and they respond to a message of hope for good jobs, renewal, and reinvestment.

An Apollo Project is attractive to swing voters, but it also heals the progressive base. By focusing on good jobs and new investment to solve persistent energy and environmental problems, Apollo offers common ground for both labor unions and environmental advocates. "By building fuel cells and wind turbines, by retooling American plants with efficient technologies, we can create good jobs, a strong economy, and a sound environment," according to Tom Buffenbarger, president of the International Association of Machinists. United Steelworkers' International's president Leo Gerard notes, "In the face of a trading system that's devastating both workers and the environment, an Apollo Project for energy independence has the potential to unite trade unionists and environmentalists in building an economy that values every worker's right to bargain for a decent living and every citizen's right to live in a healthier world."

This investment agenda is a stark contrast to Bush's millionaire tax cuts. With wealthy investors increasingly going global, Mr. Bush's tax breaks may create more jobs in Shanghai than in St. Louis. Unlike tax cuts for the rich, investment in new energy infrastructure is targeted toward and anchored in communities where it is most needed. Moreover, increasing energy efficiency provides ongoing cost savings for working families and municipal budgets. As Michael Sullivan, president of the Sheetmetal Workers' International Association says, "Energy independence means more economic security, lower energy costs, and healthier environments. The Apollo Project offers a long term solution that reinvests in communities and the future of our nation."

The pollsters Greenberg, Quinlan, and Rosner found that when asked about terrorism and events in Iraq, 86 percent of Americans placed a priority on reducing dependence on Middle East oil, with 63 percent believing that a combination of renewable power, efficient technology, and conservation is the answer to improving security. By linking national security and good jobs, and by speaking to Bush's vulnerability on the environment, clean energy will have major influence in the coming debates.

When labor and environmentalists work together, we can accomplish great things. Both movements represent real capacity for our democracy. Both bring foot soldiers, message operations, policy sophistication, and a core set of values that strengthen civil society, public welfare, and community integrity. And, both will be involved in building a solution to our country's deep economic and environmental troubles. Apollo helps forge a single progressive movement— a movement for good jobs *and* energy independence, that brings together the 14 million union members, with the 12 million environmental members, and growing majority of Americans who are concerned with the fight for civil rights and economic justice. This is a coalition that can take back power and demand a future that is both just and sustainable.

By uniting a broad coalition of labor unions, environmentalists, civil rights activists, social justice advocates, and others, the new Apollo Project showcases the best of the

Progressive movement. It restores faith in a positive role for government, and aligns activists around a common agenda built on common interests. From the railroads, to the national highway system, from Roosevelt's New Deal, to the space program, to the telecommunications revolution, visionary public leadership—and meaningful public investment— have always paved the way for great national endeavors. It is time once again to meet our challenges head on, with bold vision, a sense of optimism, and a shared commitment. It is time for a new Apollo Project for good jobs and energy independence that rebuilds America, and makes the greening of the economy the next great engine of jobs and growth.

SECTION V

SECURITY IN A CHANGING WORLD

CHAPTER 9
Preventive Democracy,
Not the Empire of Fear

The Bush administration responded to the worst act of terror on U.S. soil on September 11 by announcing its doctrine of preventive war—and launching a war first against the Taliban in Afghanistan and then, in spite of the opposition of the United Nations, traditional allies, and a broad swath of opinon at home and abroad, a "war of choice" against Iraq. At home, the administration demanded the Congress pass the Orwellian-named "Patriot Act," handing over broad new powers to search, arrest, and surveil Americans. After opposing the concept for months, the Bush administration suddenly embraced the Department of Homeland Security, and made Democratic opposition to exempting it from normal worker rights into a national security scandal for the 2002 elections. Only in recent months have the dangers and the costs of its Rambo postures become apparent.

Politically, September 11 boosted Bush's popularity, as Americans looked to their president to respond. Now, mired in Iraq, with the military overstretched, and America increasingly isolated, Americans are beginning to have doubts about the president's course. Political pundits argue that Democrats must show they are "muscular" abroad, willing to use force to defend Americans, if they are to compete for the presidency. Surely, the question of how to make America safe will be a central theme of the next months. Here, drawn from the Take Back America Conference, are two

*addresses on foreign policy, which suggest elements of a bold pro-
gressive alternative.*

A REAL SECURITY AGENDA
by Benjamin Barber

WE ARE HERE TO "take back America." But the America we
fight to reclaim is no longer just ours. In the new world of
interdependence, it belongs to the world, in whose name it
must be repossessed. Not that this is President Bush's
agenda. He appears to thinks the world belongs to America.
Which puts George Bush and his administration and the
America they affect to represent, on a collision course with
history.

The goal is to achieve security in a world of chaos and terrorism without surrendering liberty. The question is how
that is to be done without denying the new realities of interdependence.

The Bush administration has chosen to do it by military
means and to do it alone—multilateral where possible, but
unilateral wherever necessary. With United Nations support
if easy and costless, otherwise in spite of the United
Nations. And so, in confronting terrorism and prosecuting
wars abroad and security at home, this administration has
conjured the very fear that is terrorism's principal weapon.
For fear is a product of imagination. Terrorists, otherwise
bereft of power, have bored into the American mind and
seeded its recesses and crannies with anxieties for which the
Technicolor terror-alert codes are our new TV goblins.

The trouble with this militant unilateralist approach to security is that it cannot and will not work in the real world in which America is seeking to survive—perhaps even to flourish. Instead, insulated from the Old World by two centuries of near-mythic independence, but stunned today by a sudden consciousness of vulnerability, the administration is clearly failing to read the message of mandatory interdependence that defines the new twenty-first-century world. Bush's hawks pursue a reckless militancy aimed at establishing an American empire of fear more awesome than any the terrorists can conceive. They are promising to disarm every adversary, to deploy the mother of all bombs, to remove the taboo against the tactical use of nuclear weapons, to strike first, not second, to "shock and awe" enemies and friends alike into global submission. The beacon of democracy the world once most admired has abruptly become the maker of war the world most fears.

To be sure, there are those who think this is all to the good. The issue for America and the world alike is not only whether America can deploy new strategies of preventive war and still stay true to its defining democratic values, but also whether these strategies can actually succeed in securing it against terrorism. The fibs and lies and fabrications aside, the only reasonable rationale for the wars in Afghanistan and Iraq was to combat terror. After all, no nation can be expected to sacrifice its safety on the altar of its nobler aspirations. Machiavelli taught the prince it was better to be feared than loved and President Bush's hawks have taken this lesson to heart.

Yet scaring the other side into submission through a

demonstration of overwhelming American might against adversaries who may or may not have linkages to terrorism but whose defeat manifests American resolve and willingness to take on every potential enemy has also wrapped Americans in a cocoon of fear. Passive spectators to Bush's wars, Americans can more easily feel the trepidation and dependency of unwilling witnesses to some patron's well-meant war than the courage and resolve of citizen-soldiers participating in the battle. To be sure, when the War on Terrorism was first declared, many Americans hoped to participate in its sacrifices. Action and engagement were intuitively understood to be the keys to overcoming fear. Yet we were told not to worry—to reclaim normalcy and head back to the mall. This is the first war in history funded by tax cuts, the first driven by a patriotism incarnated in the act of shopping. Starting with Kuwait, and on to Afghanistan and Iraq, this is the first era in which democracy's wars are being fought by a professional army made up of those least represented in the democracy for which they are fighting, and where the citizens being protected are insulated from even the indirect costs of war.

Secretary Rumsfeld has said that citizen-soldiers are inadequate to the demands of smart war in all its technological splendor. Yet the rationale for citizens serving in war is grounded in democracy itself, and is not to be dismissed by technical considerations. War is always democracy's last resort, and in order to keep it that way, citizens are asked to make the ultimate sacrifice in common. Without the conscript army of the 1960s, America might still be in Vietnam today. With only a single member of Congress with a child serving in the military today, congressional support for war unending has become frighteningly unproblematic. When Congressman Charles Rangel suggested that if America was to fight an endless war against terrorism, it ought to reintroduce the draft, his plea was dismissed as a political ploy. In truth it conjured an apparently unwelcome vision of the true meaning of democratic sovereignty where citizens both decide for war and peace and then take direct responsibility for their decisions. War without citizens is tantamount to democracy without citizens, which is no democracy at all.

This is not to say America does not require a national security policy, or that isolationism, pacifism, or mere goodwill suffice to establish such a policy. But even the administration has acknowledged that its new enemies are "stateless martyrs" (Rumsfeld) with neither conventional interests to be negotiated nor a conventional address to which deterrent threats can be sent. Terrorists are not states, not even rogue states; and overthrowing tyrannical regimes, even where they can be shown to host terrorists, will not destroy terrorism. For terrorism is a mobile parasite that moves from one host body to another, and the destruction of one host in Afghanistan or Iraq leads only to a further dispersion of the parasite to other hosts (Syria? Iran? Sudan? Indonesia? the Philippines? New Jersey?).

Preventive war must be waged against terrorists directly, but cannot be justified against sovereign states, which are appropriate candidates for deterrence and containment (which was in fact how the Bush team dealt with Saddam Hussein prior to the war). An appropriate preventive democracy military strategy targets terrorists rather than states, and utilizes international law and multilateral cooperation as its tools. Intelligence and police cooperation have already done more to net terrorists around the world than the two costly wars in which America has engaged. But such cooperation depends on collaboration and goodwill, and cannot be imposed on others by brute military force.

The great virtue of preventive democracy as an antiterrorist strategy is that it rests on our strengths—law, cooperation, internationalism, transparency, and self-government; whereas preventive war plays out on the turf of our adversaries, the turf of fear. America today seems, in many ways, a nation beset by fear. The Bush government uses fear to make its case for war, to dub its critics traitors, to silence dissent, to pervert the meaning of patriotism, to justify agencies like the Total Information Awareness Agency (now terminated by an alarmed Congress) that would destroy our privacy and destroy our dignity. If we Americans cannot find our way out of fear's empire—since fear is about perception, not reality—the terrorists win without firing another shot. When the administration manipulates fear by conjuring dangers that cannot be specified but are said to be unavoidable, when the terror alert codes bounce up and down in scarily whimsical ways based on private interpretations of private intelligence data, when it is announced that there *will* be a terrorist event utilizing weapons of mass destruction sometime soon by someone not yet know to us at someplace where crowds gather but otherwise unspecifiable, homeland security is not enhanced and terrorism is not stymied. Rather, fear is aroused, and the terrorist's work is done for them. To fight fear with fear is to allow the invasive terrorist microbe to leverage our immune system to its advantage. It would be a sad irony if America were destroyed not by terrorism but by its own hyper-reaction to terrorism. Preventive democracy utilizes our virtues rather than our vices to take on terrorism, changing the environment that makes terrorism possible while enhancing America's own virtues.

Most Americans are in fact a good deal less afraid than the administration and the craven media would make them. Perhaps they recognize that America cannot at once be as powerful as it boasts, and as vulnerable as it fears. Terrorism is a function of powerlessness, and hurts the powerful only as they allow themselves to be hurt. Democracy defeats terrorism because democracy makes imagination into a tool of empathy, and empowers citizens here and overseas to act rather than watch, so they cannot be taken in by fear's grim games. If spectatorship means passivity and a sense of vulnerability, citizenship means action and a sense of empowerment. The logic of liberty and the logic of security are linked through the instrumentality of citizenship.

Preventive war cannot overcome terror, preventive democracy can. It empowers those whom terrorism would victimize and makes them relatively immune to the power of terrorism. But when extended to the powerless, it also empowers those who dwell on the margins in despair and anger—those whose rage and humiliation give power to terrorism. Preventive democracy prevents terrorism by empowering people and making the reliance on self-destructive violence unnecessary and counterproductive.

In the United States, the democratic deficit is worsened by the reliance on preventive war. That is manifest in what may be regarded as our two competing national anthems. *The Star Spangled Banner*, penned by Francis Scott Key watching the British bombardment of Baltimore in 1812, is the official anthem and has long been the martial coda of a sovereign and proudly independent United States, self-reliant and omnipotent, a collectivist Lone Ranger capable of imposing justice worldwide by dint of its own military hegemony. But there is also *America the Beautiful*, written by the poet Katharine Lee Bates as she gazed up at the front range of the soaring Rockies in 1893, a hymn reflecting democratic virtues which speaks to an America that acknowledges its interdependence and embraces the world to which it belongs. Bates was a practiced critic of America's first age of imperialism at the end of the nineteenth century, and she knew the secret of liberty's preservation. In the less-known second verse of her anthem, she wrote:

> *America! America!*
> *God mend thine every flaw,*
> *Confirm thy soul in self-control,*
> *Thy liberty in law!*

Dwight Eisenhower—it often seems to be the generals who know the truth about war—said forty years ago that Americans must recognize there can be no peace without law and that there can be no law if we invoke one code of international conduct for those who oppose us, and another for ourselves and our friends.

Our choice today is between invoking and obeying the international law that must girdle our anarchic interdependence or defying it as fearsomely as the terrorists have done. It is a choice to live under fear's empire or deny its sovereignty over us, a choice to cultivate smart children rather than smart bombs, a choice for preventative democracy over preventative war. To choose preventive democracy will be to embrace with new affirmative forms of democratic governance the interdependence that already governs our lives—if only in malevolent ways through predatory global capital, ecological disasters, global health plagues like HIV, SARS, and the West Nile virus, criminal activity in drugs, prostitutions, child pornography, and the international weapons trade, and—of course—terrorism. America will be stronger, not weaker, when it embraces the interdependence under which we all necessarily live. Going it alone may flatter America's "patriots" or it may appall America's moralists. But the real difficulty is it does not and cannot effectively secure America against terrorism or the other looming plagues of interdependence. America has proved it can make war alone, but it has also proved it cannot alone make peace or forge democracy in the anarchic aftermath of war. Prevention in an interdependent world is a common task which no nation, however powerful, can achieve by itself.

On the way to a fresh foreign policy based on preventive democracy and the recognition of interdependence, an international coterie of citizens has adopted a new "Declaration of Interdependence" which will be promulgated on September 12, 2003, the first "Interdependence Day" to be celebrated in Philadelphia and Budapest as well as in schools and universities in many places (for details see www.civworld.org). The Declaration reads as follows:

DECLARATION OF INTERDEPENDENCE

We the people of the world do herewith declare our interdependence as individuals and members of distinct communities and nations. We do pledge ourselves citizens of one CivWorld, civic, civil and civilized. Without prejudice to the goods and interests of our national and regional identities, we recognize our responsibilities to the common goods and liberties of humankind as a whole.

We do therefore pledge to work both directly and through the nations and communities of which we are also citizens:

To guarantee justice and equality for all by establishing on a firm basis the human rights of every person on the planet, ensuring that the least among us may enjoy the same liberties as the prominent and the powerful;

To forge a safe and sustainable global environment for all—which is the condition of human survival—at a cost to peoples based on their current share in the world's wealth;

To offer children, our common human future, special attention and protection in distributing our common goods, above all those upon which health and education depend;

To establish democratic forms of global civil and legal governance through which our common rights can be secured and our common ends realized;
    and

To foster democratic policies and institutions expressing and protecting our human commonality;
>   and at the same time,
To nurture free spaces in which our distinctive religious, ethnic and cultural identities may flourish and our equally worthy lives may be lived in dignity, protected from political, economic and cultural hegemony of every kind.

Interdependence Day falls on September 12, the day after the memorial to that fateful day on September 11, 2001, when terrorism came to America and changed the course of history by teaching us that unless all are free and equal, none may be free and equal. Unless the poorest most desperate nations find a way to live democratically, the world's oldest democracies may perish. Declaring our interdependence and celebrating the possibility of rendering interdependence just and democratic for all is one way to begin the struggle to take back America by joining the world.

DOONESBURY © 2003 G. B. Trudeau. Reprinted with permission of UNIVERSAL PRESS SYNDICATE. All rights reserved.

CHAPTER 10
The Cost of Choosing War

How do we make Americans safe in a chaotic world after September 11? That challenge will be a centerpiece of our national political debate and policy struggle over the next years. President Bush's doctrine of pre-emptive war—launching wars of choice "before the threat emerges"—has shown its costs in Iraq. Here, Tom Andrews, leader of the Win Without War Coalition that opposed the Iraq War, explores an alternative path.

SECURITY IN A CHANGED WORLD
by Tom Andrews

IF YOU ASK OUR friends and allies around the world as I have: "What is the single most important thing that we as Americans can do to advance a just and secure world?" They will say—with conviction and virtual unanimity—"defeat George W. Bush!"

They are right. We will not be able to achieve genuine security at home or abroad unless George W. Bush is defeated in November of 2004.

The sober reality is, however, that George Bush will be re-elected—and we will be subjected to four more years of an extraordinarily reckless and dangerous foreign policy—unless we are able and willing to challenge a national security strategy that is a threat to not only the values and principles that we cherish, but to the safety and security of our country and our planet.

Some argue that since the American public tends to favor the Bush administration and the Republican Party on foreign policy and national security issues—and since the Democratic party remains divided on these issues—Democratic candidates for public office in 2004 should stick to nondefense areas such as health care, education, and the economy where they enjoy an advantage.

I argue that they are wrong. Ignoring national security issues is a grave error for anyone seeking public office in 2004. A Democratic candidate could win the day on education, health care, jobs, and any number of important issues, but if the American electorate believes that the Bush administration and its Republican allies are the best hope for keeping America safe, they will re-elect the president and keep a Republican Congress, period.

Progressives, therefore, have a grave responsibility to present a vigorous and sustained political challenge to the radical militaristic policies of the Bush administration and the neoconservatives that direct them. And we have a further obligation to present to the American people a clear, compelling, and credible alternative to those policies.

We have two important assets:

Number one, we have a highly committed base of support, starting with those who marched against the invasion and occupation of Iraq, whether in the streets of cities and towns around the nation or by "virtually marching" on the offices of their congressional delegation. They represent a powerful force that—if directed toward focused and political action—can make a major difference.

Secondly, we have a large number of what pollsters call "persuadable" voters who opposed the invasion before it began. While there were significant numbers of these voters who indicated support for the Iraq invasion once it began, this was largely an expression of their support for our troops and the commander-in-chief. Many of them have grave misgivings not only about a long-term occupation of Iraq but many of the other features of the Bush administration's unilateral militarism.

Our mission is to inform, energize, and mobilize our base while we reach, repeatedly and relentlessly, those persuadables who are open to our message—particularly those who live in the "swing states" that will determine who will be elected to the White House in 2004.

Let us be clear. This is a dangerous world. There are enormous and growing threats to our national security:

1. Poverty and hopelessness, along with the repression of autocratic regimes that tolerate no peaceful dissent (including the many regimes that we actively support) are fertile ground for the seeds of terrorism. The widening gap between the haves and have-nots, the global north and south, and the misery, hopelessness, and frustration that it breeds are a threat to everyone's security.

2. The spread of global epidemics including the scourge of AIDS, whose victims are allowed to die of both a

horrible disease and a failed health-care system driven all too often not by the Hippocratic oath, but by the bottom line.

3. The relentless assault on our environment that is most acute in the global South as unfettered multi-national corporations take advantage of vast natural resources, desperate economies, and corrupt regimes.

4. Civil unrest and civil war—such as that in the Congo that has claimed over 3.3 million lives out of a population of 54 million.

5. The spread of weapons of mass destruction and the vulnerability of urban societies to even homemade conventional weapons.

The list intentionally focuses on the root causes of instability, fustration, and anger that fuel terrorism. No national security strategy is complete without seriously addressing these root causes. The Bush administration slights this effort, focusing instead upon a military response. But we must not be deluded. The United States will find far greater security in the world if it is seen as a source of hope rather than a source of fear or oppression.

But too often, when we focus on the root conditions of terror, we slight the need to address—in clear and convincing ways—the fears and anxieties that most immediately grip Americans, and for which they demand answers, *now*.

The past two years have been marked by color-coded alert levels. The airwaves are full of talk of threat about terrorists engineering new diseases without a cure or disseminating deadly agents through air-ventilation systems. Health workers are encouraged to get smallpox vaccines. Cities engage in elaborate drills to practice for an attack. The President wages war and occupies another country because, he says, it poses a grave danger to us. Fanatical suicide bombers are part of today's reality. We hear about the hostile, irrational, and fanatical North Korean leadership brazenly pursuing nuclear weapons in defiance of the United States and the rest of world. Conflicts simmering in South Asia and the Middle East threaten to pull us in.

No wonder countless Americans today feel insecure and worry not just about their jobs, health, and financial security, but also about their physical security.

We have an obligation to tell the American people how and why the reckless policies of the Bush administration are undermining our security. Or, to ask the American people—similar to the way that Ronald Reagan asked them in his campaign for president against Jimmy Carter: "Are we safer today than we were before the military invasion and occupation of Iraq?"

ARE WE SAFER TODAY THAN WE WERE BEFORE THE IMPLEMENTATION OF THE BUSH ADMINISTRATION'S "NATIONAL SECURITY STRATEGY"?

The U.S. invasion and occupation of Iraq turns out to be a trial run in what this administration calls a "new norm" in international relations. This new norm is the doctrine of preventive war that the administration announced explicitly in its National Security Strategy last fall and which it has expounded on since. It holds that the United States has the right to attack *any* country that it claims to be a potential threat—not an actual threat, or an imminent threat—but a *potential* threat. The new strategy stresses offensive military intervention, preemptive first strikes, and proactive counter proliferation measures against so-called rogue states and other enemies. By rejecting the notion of working within international law, as well as the policies of deterrence and collective security, the Bush administration is pursuing a vision in which the United States is not only the world's policeman, but also the world's military dictator, answerable only to itself.

THE QUESTION THAT EVERY AMERICAN DESERVES AN ANSWER TO IS: "DOES THE INVASION OF IRAQ AND THIS 'NEW NORM' OF THE BUSH NATIONAL SECURITY STRATEGY, MAKE AMERICA SAFER?"

Let's start with the lessons that other nations, including those we call the "axis of evil," are taking from this trial run of the "new norm" in international relations—the invasion and occupation of Iraq. The administration believes that it will serve as a cautionary tale—*one false move and you will suffer the fate of the Iraqi leadership.* Well, the fact is that it is having precisely the *opposite* effect. Indeed, the real message to other nations is: *You had better develop nuclear weapons, or other weapons of mass destruction immediately, or you too will be vulnerable to a United States "preventive war."*

This is what North Korea's foreign ministry had to say after the invasion of Iraq began: "To allow disarmament through inspections does not help avert a war, but rather sparks it." The statement concludes, with unerring logic, that "only a tremendous military deterrent force" can prevent attacks on states the United States dislikes.

DOES THIS MAKE AMERICA AND THE WORLD SAFER?

And what if the doctrine of preemption—that holds that one nation can attack another if it believes that the other nation poses a *potential* threat to its security—is embraced by bitter enemies with their fingers on the trigger of nuclear weapons, like India and Pakistan? What if it is embraced by North Korea?

DOES THIS MAKE AMERICA AND THE WORLD SAFER?

The fact is that the administration will find that North Korea, with its massive arsenal pointed at Seoul, is not such easy prey for U.S. military might. And it will find that Iran's nuclear program cannot be stopped by attacking its facilities—many of which we can't even locate—and that there is no chance that Iranians would welcome U.S. troops as liberators.

The Bush doctrine rests on the notion that the American public will accept the costs and risks of an American military empire and the United States as world cop.

Before the invasion of Iraq, the administration was reluctant to discuss what the invasion would lead to—a full-scale occupation for an indeterminate amount of time at an indeterminate cost. Nor was it willing to talk about the fact that, unlike the first Gulf War—that was sanctioned by the UN Security Council and where 90 percent of its costs were paid by our allies—the American people will have to shoulder at least 90 percent of the monetary costs of the invasion and occupation of Iraq. This is not to mention the ongoing loss of American lives due to the extraordinary arrogance and shortsightedness of the administration when it came to occupying—as a military power—this desperate and volatile country.

President Bush took our nation to war based on two specious arguments. One claim was that this war was necessary because Iraq's weapons of mass destruction were a potential threat. The president and his administration told the American people repeatedly about Iraq's vast weapons programs, with thousands of tons of chemical and biological weapons that could kill millions of people. U.S. and British forces have now occupied the entire country for months. They have failed to turn up evidence of any chemical or biological weapons, let alone massive programs. The Iraqi regime's failure to use any such weapons, even at the point of its own destruction, argues that either they do not have any usable biological or chemical weapons or they concluded their use would be ineffective. *Whatever the reality, it demonstrates that a tough inspection regime, given time and resources, could have adequately addressed the threat posed by Iraq's weapons programs.*

The second claim was that the United States was combating terrorism by overthrowing Saddam Hussein and occupying the country. The president and his administration repeatedly spoke of Iraq and September 11 almost in the same breath. American soldiers reportedly inscribed the names of September 11 victims on the missiles and bombs they launched against hapless Iraqi conscripts, buildings, homes, and marketplaces.

I would like to read you a quote from a mother of Capt. Tristan Aitken, a U.S. soldier who lost his life eleven days ago in Iraq:

> He was doing his job. He had no choice, and I'm proud of who he was. But it makes me mad that this whole war was sold to the American public and to the soldiers as something it wasn't. Our forces have been convinced that Iraqis were responsible for September 11, and that's not true.

Of course, she is right. It is well documented that the plan for "regime change" in Iraq predated September 11. The terrorist attacks on that day provided the "neocons" driving the Bush administration foreign policy the political opening they needed to engage their new national security strategy. And now, after the fact, the president has admitted that Iraq had nothing to do with the September 11 attacks.

The more time goes by the clearer it becomes that the invasion of Iraq was based on a lie—about al Qaeda, about weapons of mass destruction, about the costs of occupation, about the enormous risks, and the consequences of defying international opinion and law.

The most important decision that a government can make—the life-and-death decision of war and peace—cannot be based on a lie. The Bush administration and its allies in Congress need to be held accountable. Their deception and manipulation of the American people not only led to an unnecessary and illegal attack on a sovereign nation, it was an attack on democracy itself. For democracy to work, citizens must have accurate information with which to engage in an open debate about the policy decisions that affect their lives. Americans were systematically denied this information in the days and weeks leading to the invasion of Iraq. Through the manipulation of intelligence data, the repetition of baseless claims, the presentation of "facts" that were patently false and the persistent use of fear, the administration attacked the fundamentals of democracy itself while sinking our nation into a dangerous quagmire.

This gang knows how to break things, but it doesn't know how to build something better in its place. Afghanistan and Iraq are exhibits A and B. It has no apparent strategy to build bridges to moderates in Iran or to reach an agreement with North Korea and turn toward the day when North and South Korea are one. It shows little understanding of the need to address the conditions—including U.S. policies—that fuel terrorism, of the need to "drain that swamp" that allows terrorism to grow as opposed to the silly notion that the United States can simply "hunt 'em down, one by one."

Perhaps some found comfort or satisfaction in the belief that the United States was responding to the evil of September 11 when it invaded Iraq. But, we should not be deluded into thinking that we have struck a blow against terrorism. *Genuine progress against international terrorism has been made possible not by the Bush Doctrine, but by international cooperation and coordination.* The proof can be found in the successful campaign to track down and capture key al Qaeda operatives. European governments, Pakistan, and others are responsible for the most significant achievements in apprehending suspected terrorists and disrupting their plans. The battle against terrorism cannot be waged effectively without intelligence from other countries, international law enforcement operations, and worldwide coordination to shut down financial support that flows to the terrorists. Alienating the international community and building resentment with a go-it-alone foreign policy threatens what we know works to rein in terrorism and keep Americans and the world safer.

While Arabs do not mourn Saddam's passing, they do not welcome occupation of a sovereign Islamic state by a western military power. As expected, the war has caused an upsurge in anti-American sentiment in the Middle East—and around the world. Al Qaeda was created and became empowered by the U.S. presence in Saudi Arabia following the first Gulf War. What new networks will be spawned in reaction to the U.S. presence in Iraq? What can we expect from the tens of thousands of Iraqi children whose parents or siblings were killed by their so-called liberators? Egyptian leader Hosni Mubarak, a friend of the United States, predicted last week that this war would produce "a hundred [Osama] bin Ladens."

The administration has brought about regime change as promised. But the world will judge its performance in fulfilling its far more demanding promises: to rebuild the cities we've just destroyed, restore order in the chaos of the vacuum we created, meet the pressing and overwhelming humanitarian needs, and promote democracy, not just in Iraq, but in the region. It is obvious to us that a lead role for the UN and outside relief agencies in reconstruction is required if this effort is to be seen as legitimate. Just as it is obvious that the president's words will ring hollow if the United States anoints Iraq's next leaders, or continues unabated its support for autocratic regimes throughout the Middle East, or, most significantly, does not promptly make genuine and sustained efforts to promote a just peace between Israel and the Palestinians.

Recent developments are not encouraging. The decision to run Iraq out of the Pentagon, complete with the handing out of no-bid contracts to politically connected firms like Halliburton, undermines U.S. claims that we are nation builders, not occupiers. The fact that many humanitarian organizations will not operate under U.S. military command is delaying desperately needed humanitarian aid. And how will any Iraqi government—even an interim one—be able to gain the authority and legitimacy that it will need, if it is brought to power by being anointed exclusively by the United States?

One of the tasks of the antiwar movement is to keep the spotlight on the United States's obligations as an occupying power. Its track record is not promising. A year and a half after the cheering in Kabul has died down, rival warlords are back ruling most of Afghanistan with widespread torture, Taliban-style repression, rampant lawlessness, and a revival of the drug trade.

Those of us who opposed the war on Iraq have a tough and critical job to do. With a Congress that has abdicated its responsibility to provide checks and balances on the administration, and the UN having been cast aside, Win Without War and the citizens' movement of this country are more important than ever. Unless we are willing to engage, inform, and mobilize our base of sympathetic Americans and reach those who are open to our message, Americans may very well find themselves at war again. We are talking about future wars that are avoidable, that fuel terrorism, that isolate us from historic allies—whose cooperation we need to fight terrorism effectively—that undermine the rule of law, that heap enormous costs of the American people alone, that serve as partial justification for the suspension of civil liberties and that make all Americans less secure.

Martin Luther King once said, "I do not believe our nation can be a moral leader of justice, equality, and democracy if it is trapped in the role of a self-appointed world policeman." He was right.

What are we to do? Well, for starters, at least two things:

1. We must commit ourselves to a public campaign that relentlessly challenges the administration—starting with the reality that Americans are less safe as a result of the Bush Doctrine and the arrogance, ignorance and deception that led us into the quagmire of Iraq. We must present a coherent and compelling vision of a national security policy that affirms the best of our values—including respect for the truth and international law—while pursuing cooperative and coordinated international strategies to confront the threat of terrorism and the underlying conditions that allow it to thrive.

2. Launch a focused and sophisticated electoral campaign that includes both nonpartisan public education

and political components. It should be based on the need to increase the turnout of our base of support while developing well researched messages to voters who have been identified as "persuadable" and who live in key political venues; delivering these messages through targeted media venues and sustained grass-roots outreach campaigns; and maximizing the turnout of these voters to the polls.

At another pivotal time of crisis for our nation, Abraham Lincoln said, "The dogmas of the quiet past are inadequate to the stormy present. As our case is new, so must we think anew and act anew. We must disenthrall ourselves and then we shall save our country."

It is time to disenthrall ourselves from the notion that we cannot or that we should not address national security issues head-on in the days, weeks, and months heading into the 2004 election.

Our nation can have a national security strategy that reflects the best of who we are while making us—and the citizens of the world—more secure; and we can translate the enormous power and energy so vividly displayed by citizens from every walk of life in cities and towns across the nation in the days before the invasion of Iraq, into a powerful and sustained political force that can transform our nation.

Let us tap the energy, enthusiasm, and wisdom that abounds at this gathering and together, take back our nation. There is no choice.

SECTION VI

EXPANDING DEMOCRACY

CHAPTER 11
Holding Corporations Accountable

One cornerstone of the right-wing agenda for America is a concerted attack on "trial lawyers," depicting them as a threat to the economy, to prosperity, to health care, to safe streets. "Tort reform"—essentially efforts to free corporations from liability for negligence or willful destructive acts and to limit the ability of their victims to collect damages from them— is at the top of the president's agenda—and a centerpiece of his fundraising appeals. Below, one of America's most feared and eminent trial lawyers reminds us of the need for accountability.

AMERICAN LAW:
INSTRUMENT OF SOCIAL PROGRESS
OR WEAPON OF REPRESSION?[*]
William S. Lerach

WHEN I WENT TO law school, most of us viewed American law as an instrument for positive change. We were then still in the wake of the historic 1938 amendments to the Federal Rules which simplified civil litigation to make justice more accessible to all litigants, large and small. In those days, civil

---

[*] Adapted from Commencement Address, Pennsylvania Law School, May 2003.

suits seemed to be promoting remarkable changes in our society—changes that many of us believe were for the good.

During much of my life in the law, I have seen how individuals, aided by courageous advocates, in exercising their access to our courts and by vindicating their own rights, were able to stimulate change that never could have been accomplished legislatively. The law was a dynamic force for positive change—driven by lawyers who cared.

There is no better example than *Brown vs. The Board of Education,* a class action suit by black parents and their children—aided by brave lawyers—who used our civil justice system to obtain their admission to segregated schools. They thereby helped to desegregate all our public schools, overturning decades of shameful legal precedent. Their suit forced fundamental progress that was impossible to achieve through legislative action, because those with political power prevented any change.

I also recall *Baker vs. Carr,* another landmark class action which challenged the entrenched control of state legislatures by rural legislators, who drew legislative districts based on acres—but not people—perpetuating their own political control while denying to millions of American voters their right of equal representation. Again, private suits brought about a fundamental and more equitable redistribution of political power that never could have been achieved through the legislative process.

How about *Griswold vs. Connecticut,* where lawyers were able to overturn state laws that were nothing more than the repressive exercise of religious power and dogma and begin the process by which Americans could intelligently engage in family planning and indulge their sexuality. And then lawyers prevailed in *Rowe vs. Wade*—the class action suit by which American women took their reproductive processes back from male- and religiously-dominated state legislatures.

There are many more examples.

I can still remember when many consumer products seemed more a hazard than a benefit . . . The automobiles of my youth . . . were deathtraps. Exposed gas tanks. No airbags. Not even seatbelts. Rigid steering wheels and columns that crushed or impaled countless drivers. Fragile windshields that decapitated or scarred countless victims . . . It was civil litigation—and the financial exposure of the powerful auto companies—that exposed these defects and drove the auto industry to make safer cars.

Another example is medical malpractice litigation. You don't remember when "sponges" were regularly left in surgical patients because doctors were not concerned enough to count them. Wrong limbs were, if not regularly, all too frequently amputated. Serious medication errors were so frequent that hospitalization became a bet-your-life experience. But as mistreated patients held medical providers legally responsible for these grotesque mistakes, no one can dispute that the quality of medical care improved.

And there is the tobacco industry. Citizens enraged at this oligopoly of death filed suits that ended the infamous "Joe Camel" advertising campaign, which was so effective in enticing youngsters to begin smoking. And it was civil suits, not legislative action, that exposed the secret industry documents showing how craven executives targeted our children with products that they knew were as addictive as heroin to get them hooked...The fact that today it is the cigarette industry that is crippled . . . is due to results obtained by courageous lawyers in civil suits—not any government legislation. The industry's power could not stop empowered citizens fighting in court to redress wrongs.

But the benefits from socially committed lawyers were not confined to desegregating schools, assuring equal voting, protecting sexual freedom and reproductive choice, forcing corporations to make safer products and challenging their miscreant behavior. Courageous lawyering has also been very important in enforcing the constitutional rights of our citizens.

It was lawyers . . . who overturned repressive precedents that allowed police searches and arrests on the flimsiest grounds and denied individuals who found themselves at the mercy of a powerful state criminal justice system any warning concerning their constitutional rights or even the assistance of a lawyer to help them understand the legal procedures upon which their liberty . . . depended. Were it not for decisions obtained by lawyers representing these unpopular and powerless accused persons, our right to counsel, guarantees of privacy and restraints on police searches and seizures would have little real meaning today.

There are, of course, many more examples . . . but I hope I have made the point. When I studied here, and for many of the years I have been practicing, it seemed to be accepted that the ability of individuals to use their access to the courts to seek an adjudication of their individual grievances or to have a chance to defend themselves not only ensured civil and criminal justice to those individuals, but was healthy for society as a whole. Adam Smith's invisible hand motivated entrepreneurial lawyers like me to identify and prosecute suits against corporations that cared more about profits than people. Idealistic public-interest, criminal-defense and often volunteer lawyers helped defendants ensnared in our criminal system try to protect themselves. And over time, these suits and legal challenges forced changes that benefited all of us.

One would think that these lawyers, if not hailed as heroes, would at least not be condemned as villains. But today, increasingly, they are. Change brings disruption. Frederick Douglas said "power concedes nothing without a struggle." And it is too easy today to forget the struggle that seemed to be bringing us a more humane, even-handed legal system.

So now I must address changes of the last several years in our legal system which alarm me. For most of its history, the law has been an instrument of the rich, the powerful and the state to serve their ends—a weapon of repression. I fear that before our very eyes—but with too few of us seeing it—American law is being transmogrified back into that weapon of repression. Something very troubling has happened. Lawyers who speak for the underprivileged, the minorities, the injured, even the outcasts, are today reviled. Their legal challenges are not viewed as the legitimate expression, or protection, of individual rights, but rather as exploitive tools utilized by avaricious, immoral "mouthpieces" to line their own pockets—even as dirty tricks to protect the guilty from their just desserts.

Listen to claims made by a famous political leader who wanted to curtail the ability of lawyers to protect the legal rights of his fellow citizens: Every lawyer "must be regarded as a man deficient by nature, or else deformed by usage." Lawyers are "idiots" and "absolute cretins."

"The lawyer's profession is essentially unclean." He even promised: "To make every [citizen] realize that it is a disgrace to be a lawyer."

I'll tell you the speaker's name later. But sadly, because of attitudes like these, American law is in danger of returning to a tool of repression. I offer a few examples.

In the 1980s and 90s, lawyers in securities fraud class action suits recovered billions for cheated investors. They called to account the financial psychopath Charles Keating and his corrupt lawyers, accountants and investment bankers, recovering $250 million for fleeced elderly retirees. Other suits exposed junk bond king Michael Milken and Drexel Burnham—recovering billions for the victims of their criminal enterprise. Lawyers recovered over $750 million for victims sold worthless bonds to finance a boondoggle known as the Washington Public Power Supply System. And when we caught the Wall Street operations fixing the prices of stock trades, another billion dollars was recovered for investors. Thus did lawyers vindicate the rights of wronged investors and help police our securities markets as private attorneys general.

But, as they say, no good deed goes unpunished. Ironically, because of these suits, corporate and Wall Street interests and the accounting oligopoly went to Congress for assistance. And Congress caved. New laws enacted in 1995 and 1998 severely curtailed the ability of investors to sue for fraud. Private enforcement was immediately chilled. And quickly, market miscreants were emboldened. Within just a few years, our nation was awash in the greatest upsurge of financial fraud since the 1920s—a feast of cooked books and huge frauds at companies that once were respected names but are now epithets: Enron, WorldCom, Qwest, Tyco and HealthSouth. This fraud wave inflicted trillions of dollars of losses on investors and devastated investor confidence.

We also witnessed a massive manipulation of the initial public offering market by which Wall Street financiers rigged stock prices while their analysts issued phony research reports—to enrich themselves, their venture capitalist clients and favored insiders, while cheating public investors out of billions. This chicanery has contributed to massive market declines—impairing capital formation, economic growth and job creation while destroying the retirement dreams of millions of ordinary people. Scars from which our financial system has not yet even begun to recover. So much for the fruits of this recent legislative foray into that euphemism called "Tort Reform." Rarely do we see the impact of bad policy so quickly and catastrophically.

Yet, despite this debacle, today we are witnessing an unremitting assault by corporate interests on the rights of citizens to use our legal system to vindicate their rights. Consider class actions. Despite all that this uniquely American legal vehicle has allowed our ordinary people to achieve, an all-out assault on class actions is underway in the national legislature—a campaign to chloroform them—actually to kill them—that I fear may well succeed.

Today we also see an assault on medical malpractice suits that would limit the ability of victims of even the most grotesque mistakes to recover damages. It is chilling that this effort can be so brazenly pursued, notwithstanding the recent catastrophe where a top-flight medical institution transplanted mismatched organs into a youngster and killed her, because even the most rudimentary blood- and tissue-matching tests were not performed. And this assault goes on at a time when hospital medication errors remain so prevalent that the FDA has recently had to propose new extensive controls over their administration.

Will reducing the legal accountability of drug manufacturers and medical care providers improve the quality of health care? Will restricting the legal rights of people injured by defective products encourage the manufacture of safer ones? Will curtailing the ability of citizens to use class actions to call corporations to account stimulate more responsible corporate behavior? Well, did reducing corporate executives' and Wall Street financiers' accountability for securities fraud make our financial markets safer?

But it is not only the corporate interests that are waging this effort to suppress the legal rights of ordinary citizens. We face a growing assault on our rights by our own government as well. Our constitutional rights assume their greatest importance when they are most under threat. That's when they really matter. In the politically popular name of fighting terrorism, we have seen a curtailment of individual liberties not witnessed in this country in many decades. People in America can now have their communications secretly monitored and then be arrested and secretly tried for crimes that could cost them their liberty, citizenship, residence or even their lives.

I do not sanction terrorism. But if you think government will not abuse these new powers to the detriment of innocent citizens, you ignore history. Why do you think our founders created a Constitution that protected individual rights and liberty? They were very much aware of their history—of the then-recent government repression of individual expression and privacy and the inability of citizens to seek legal redress. I fear the luxury of freedom here for so long now has anesthetized many of our citizens—causing them to forget how fragile our precious liberties are. Government will take as many rights from us as we allow. And, once given up, rights are oh so much harder to reclaim.

And I cannot overlook the growing repression accompanying the death penalty. Not only is the death penalty back in business, but a few of our Southern states are death factories—at least for blacks who kill whites. This despite new powerful evidence of continuing unfairness and discrimination in capital cases. I guess it is reassuring that a defense lawyer in a capital trial is not permitted to sleep through it, but beyond that, there are few effective safeguards to protect the accused. This is something that is not without real consequence—at least to the accused—in light of the fact that new scientific tools—mostly DNA evidence—have demonstrated that we have convicted (and sadly surely executed) a large number of innocent people in recent years. In fact, so grotesquely flawed is our death penalty system today that it took a retiring Governor of Illinois—a man with no political future or need to pander—to commute the death penalties of every condemned person in his state's penal system. That's how overwhelming the evidence was there that innocent persons were being convicted in capital cases. Remember, public opinion demands that the police must solve and the prosecutors must convict in every capital case. And what needs to be done, will be done—and sometimes, the innocent be damned.

I cannot quietly accept that we live in a country where it is constitutional to execute teenagers. Where we give anti-psychotic drugs to the condemned insane to sober them up enough to march them down the hall and kill them. We now have more people on death row than any country but communist China.

I do not doubt that there are monsters for which death seems deserved. But for me, executing the innocent and teenagers and hyper-medicating the insane to kill them is simply too high a price to pay. To the economically minded among you, I say this is especially so when it costs so much more to execute than imprison for life. And to the blood-thirsty among you, I ask you which punishment is really worse—life behind bars in a tiny cell or being put to sleep by a lethal injection.

And what better example of how American law is regressing to an instrument of oppression than our Supreme Court's recent ruling that it is permissible for a state to use a three-strikes law to put a person in jail for 50 years—50 *years*—for stealing a few DVDs or golf clubs. Does that decision make you feel any safer? In my home state, we now have so many people in prison that even with a $35 billion budget deficit, we are spending five times more a year to incarcerate prisoners than we spend to educate our most precious resource—our children—$6,300 a year per student—$30,000 a year per prisoner.

I know there are differences of opinion on these issues.

Social progress for some is moral decay to others . . . My concern is that what may have started as a benign reaction to too much of a move in one direction is resulting in the very rapid swing of a very big pendulum the other way—one swinging way too fast and going way too far. I see the American law I love morphing from an instrument of social progress back into a weapon of repression. These disturbing trends have much momentum behind them. And the hour is late.

So what does all of this have to do with you? Everything. By the time you are old enough, like me, to have made enough money or done something that is sufficiently controversial to have your school ask you to come and speak, you're pretty close to the point where you're going back to the barn. People my age aren't really going to be able to do much about the troubling issues I have addressed today. But you can do everything. Because you're just beginning. In countless ways—by litigating, writing, teaching, and by shaping public opinion and legislative policies—each of you individually, and all of you collectively, will have countless opportunities to shape the American legal landscape going forward. I urge you to do what you can to return American law to an instrument of social progress and stop it from returning to a weapon of repression.

For you who care, do not think that your task will be easy. I have been lucky enough to live in a golden age of American law. But I repeat a sad truth—for most of history, in our own and in our English ancestors' legal system, the law has been a weapon of rich and powerful interests and the governments they control to suppress ordinary people in the exercise of their individual rights and liberties. If American law continues to move back into a repressive role, our whole country will be worse off. Ever more powerful corporate and financial interests and providers of indispensable services and products will be less accountable to those dependent upon them. And surely, government will arrogate for itself as much power as a passive populace—and the legal profession—will let it take.

As I close, I confess—I engaged in a little deception earlier. When I read those quotations—lawyers are "deficient by nature," "idiots," "cretins" and it is a "disgrace to be a lawyer"— which sound like comments from some of our political leaders today, I wasn't reading from the *Congressional Record*. I was actually reading from a law review article—"The Bar in the Third Reich." Those quotes were from a famous political leader by the name of Adolf Hitler. Never ever forget that the first thing Hitler did was destroy the ability of the German legal system and lawyers there to protect people, eliminating civil remedies and the constitutional protections of citizens. We have no Hitlers here today, but doesn't it say something very troubling that those quotes from 60 years ago in Nazi Germany could sound like part of today's debate here about lawyers and our legal system.

As you pursue and achieve your own success . . . please remember our American legal system can be an instrument for positive change or a weapon of repression. Which direction it takes during your generation now rests in your hands. As I go to the barn, I'll be watching and rooting for you. Good luck.

CHAPTER 12
Seizing the Continuing Moment for Democracy Reform

―――――――

As Miles Rapoport argues below, "while an election count stopped by a bare-knuckled Supreme Court once seared into our collective memory may have faded, the opportunity created by the 2000 election has exhibited remarkable staying power." Progressives need to seize this moment and win a set of reforms that can change the shape of our election system in 2004 and for the long haul. We must lead a national effort to clean up Washington, to curb the influence of money in politics, to expand the ability of candidates to present their case to the American people without being forced into an unending money chase, and to mobilize citizens to take back their government.

By Miles Rapoport

AS THE 2004 ELECTION approaches, with so much at stake for our nation, a huge amount of energy, attention, financing, and debate will focus on Election Day. But behind the political headlines is a continuing and extraordinary opportunity for reform advocates to change our democracy in ways that reverse the negative trends of previous decades, tear down barriers to participation, and make it more inclusive, vibrant, and participatory. While the images of butterfly ballots, hanging chads, thousands of African Americans turned away from the polls, and an election count stopped by a bare-knuckled Supreme Court once seared into our collective memory may have faded, the opportunity created by the 2000 election has exhibited remarkable staying power. Progressives need to seize this continuing moment to win a set of reforms that can change the shape of our election system in the near future and for the long haul.

IMPLEMENTING HAVA

The principal response from Congress to the enormous questioning of the American election process that occurred after the 2000 election was the Help America Vote Act of 2002 (HAVA). The fact that it passed, along with the Bipartisan Campaign Reform Act, in a Congress where so much valuable legislation was destroyed, is a testament to the fact that the issue of fair and democratic elections has strength and staying power. In addition, defying many predictions, Congress has already appropriated significant sums authorized by HAVA to pay for electoral reforms in the states, and appears poised to do more. Monitoring the progress of funding and of other HAVA issues in Congress will be an ongoing task. The act created a new federal Election Assistance Commission, and its four members—Gracia Hillman, Ray Martinez, Paul DeGregorio, and DeForest Soaries—were appointed on the very last day of the Congressional session in December 2003. The Commission was given very little enforcement responsibility or power, so its influence in the process is still an open question. As a result, the action around election reform has now shifted decisively to the states. Many of the implementation specifics, including the speed of change, have been left up to each state. This allows for widely varying interpretations of the federal law; thus, leaving open the possibility of either progressive reforms or regressive erosions of voting rights.

What does HAVA do specifically? HAVA mandates that all fifty states upgrade many aspects of their election procedures, including their voting machines (punch card ballots are banned), registration processes and poll worker training. It requires that each state give voters the opportunity to cast a provisional ballot if their eligibility is questioned. It requires at least one accessible machine per polling place so that voters with disabilities may cast a private ballot and mandates machinery more accessible to people with language needs. HAVA also requires the creation of a computerized, statewide voter list in every state.

For people concerned with expanding and improving our democracy, there are several problematic areas of HAVA. New voter identification requirements, which Republicans insisted upon as the price of a bipartisan bill, remain a real cause for concern. Under the law, first-time voters who register by mail must show identification—such as a driver's license or Social Security card—at the ballot box. Each state has some leverage to decide what IDs can be used. In the best states, like Ohio, election officials interpret the law broadly. They plan to accept many different kinds of IDs at the ballot box, so that no voters are needlessly turned away from the polls. In some states, however, conservative lawmakers have proposed far more rigid ID requirements in the guise of complying with HAVA, including extending the ID requirements to all voters. Civil rights advocates are monitoring the requirements that could keep many citizens from voting, especially young voters, new citizens, poor voters and voters of color.

A second area generating a great deal of attention and publicity is the issue of how well computerized voting machines can be trusted to count the ballots and whether they can be manipulated by outside hackers or unscrupulous programmers with a political agenda. The close connection of Diebold, one of the major suppliers of machinery, to the Bush administration has only heightened the concerns of many. One proposed mechanism to guarantee the accuracy of the vote count is a voter verified paper trail (VVPT). Other concerns address the openness or proprietary nature of source codes and computer instructions for the machines. State election officials and advocates need to guard carefully against the electronic manipulation of election results as they install new systems, since any efforts to achieve full voter participation will be severely hampered if people believe their votes won't even be properly counted.

On the other hand, the conversation and debate generated by HAVA and legislative changes taking place in the next several years offer democracy reform advocates the best chance in a very long time to win some real changes that can open up the process tremendously. Funding granted by HAVA can be used to support a wide variety of election reforms and improvements, while the debate itself offers a moment to advance a comprehensive reform agenda.

AN AGENDA FOR REFORM

There is no "magic bullet" to make our democracy work as it should. What ails our democracy is deep and multifaceted and requires responses on many levels. In terms of the election process itself, a number of key areas of reform have emerged as practical, achievable ways to help bring down America's barriers to voting and encourage participation. As democracy reform advocates increasingly take their battles out of D.C. and into the state legislatures, these reforms are a good place for progressives to devote resources and energy.

Election Day Registration

Election Day Registration, also known as "same day registration," allows citizens to register and vote on Election Day. Six states use EDR systems and those six states have voter participation rates 8-15 percent higher than the national average. The reason for EDR's success is simple. Many new voters get energized about an election in the last few weeks of a campaign, but most states cut off voter registration 20–30 days before an election. If new voters have not registered by then, they cannot participate and all that energy is barred from the election process. In addition, EDR allows would-be voters to cast their ballot if, for whatever reason, their name is not on the voter rolls at the polling place.

"The final week before an election—when the pressure is high, the campaign is in full swing, and the newspaper endorsements are flowing—often motivates new or undecided voters to cast their ballots if they have the opportunity to register at the polls," says Wisconsin state senator Gwendolyn Moore. She should know; her state's EDR system helped boost turnout in Wisconsin to 66 percent in 2000, 15 points higher than the national average.

Polls show that EDR appeals to people who have not

voted. In a May 2001 Medill School of Journalism poll, 64 percent of nonvoters said that allowing people to register on Election Day would make them more likely to vote. Fully 56 million eligible Americans were not even registered to vote in 2000. If an EDR system allowed 8–15 percent of those people to register and cast a ballot, it would convert millions of nonvoters into engaged citizens.

In states across the country, including California, Connecticut, New York, North Carolina, and Massachusetts concerned activists are working to pass EDR laws through ballot initiatives, legislation and advocacy. As states begin to implement the provisional voting requirements of HAVA, the eligibility of thousands of votes—in some states, tens or even hundreds of thousands—will need to be verified before being counted, causing confusion and delay. In addition, as computerized voting lists make more accurate list-maintenance the norm, the momentum for opening up registration to all on Election Day will grow.

Unlocking the Vote for Citizens with Felony Convictions

One of the largest scandals in the Florida 2000 election involved "felony disenfranchisement laws." These laws strip voting rights from people convicted of certain crimes. Thousands of Floridians with clean criminal records were purged from the voter rolls because of sloppy and overly broad purges of the voter registration database. But even more important from a democracy point of view, Florida's disenfranchisement laws kept more than 600,000 people from voting in 2000, even those who had fully finished their prison time, parole or probation. In Florida and Alabama, over 30 percent of black men are barred from voting. Across the country, almost 5 million Americans cannot vote because of criminal convictions in their past. There are no federal guidelines about these laws, so their harshness varies from state to state. The most extreme states, such as Florida, Alabama, Mississippi, Kentucky, and Virginia, bar citizens with felony convictions from voting for life.

Who are all these disenfranchised citizens? Disproportionately, they are people of color from low-income communities. Across the country, black citizens are five times more often denied the vote because of criminal records than whites. Latinos and Native Americans face similar disenfranchisement rates. This racially discriminatory effect is hardly an accident. Like poll taxes, literacy tests, and grandfather clauses, felony disenfranchisement laws were intentionally crafted in the South during Reconstruction to exclude African Americans from the political process. White lawmakers in the Jim Crow era were not shy about their intentions. "This plan" said one delegate to the Virginia convention of 1906, which established strict felony disenfranchisement laws, "will eliminate the darkey as a political factor in this state in less than five years, so that in no single county . . . will there be the least concern felt for the complete supremacy of the white race in the affairs of government."

Fortunately, the American public is ready to change these archaic, discriminatory laws. In a July 2002 Harris Interactive poll, more than 60 percent of Americans agreed that people who have completed their prison sentences should be allowed to vote; only about a quarter of disenfranchised Americans are in prison. Change is taking place in a significant number of states. Alabama, Wyoming, and Nevada all changed their laws to allow more citizens to vote in 2003. Connecticut changed its law in 2002 to allow 36,000 citizens on probation to vote. Legislation easing disenfranchisement laws has been passed in Delaware, Kentucky, Maryland, New Mexico, Pennsylvania, and Virginia. This momentum is being harnessed into a strong and broad coalition that aims to change America's felony disenfranchisement law. Like civil rights battles of the past, these changes will not be won overnight, but felony disenfranchisement laws are increasingly being recognized as barriers to democracy, and major change is on the way.

Counting Votes as They Are Intended: Instant Runoff Voting

America's heavy reliance on single-winner districts and on counting procedures that can often produce winners with a minority of votes has alienated an alarming number of voters, and produced anomalous, unintended consequences in many elections. As a result, momentum has gathered for several changes that redress this issue. A variety of solutions, including multi-representative districts, minority representation, proportional representation, and cumulative voting mechanisms, have been proposed. One reform gaining currency is Instant Runoff Voting (IRV). Under IRV, voters cast a ballot for two or more candidates, ranking them in order of preference. When the votes are counted, the candidate with the least votes is eliminated, and those votes are automatically redistributed to the voters' second preference.

Advocates of the IRV system maintain that it is clearly

preferable to a situation in which third party candidates serve as spoilers, throwing the results of an election to a candidate who does not reflect the views of a majority. For instance, in New Hampshire and Florida in 2000, an IRV system would have cast votes for Ralph Nader to the voters' second preference (likely Al Gore), rather than discounting them and pushing the victory to George Bush. In addition, supporters of minor party candidates would not be forced to choose between casting a ballot for their true choice or casting a "strategic" ballot for a candidate they liked less but who stood a better chance to win; through IRV, they can do both. In those states and municipalities that do utilize runoffs, IRV seems highly preferable to a runoff election a month later, where turnout is almost invariably a fraction of what it is in the original election. IRV has made strides in the past two years. San Francisco voters adopted IRV in March of 2002 and will first utilize it in November 2004. More than fifty Vermont towns voted for instant runoff voting through non-binding referenda in 2002 as well. In the same year, the Utah Republican Party used IRV to nominate candidates for the Congressional race.

Campaign Finance Reform: The Beginning, Not the End

The Supreme Court has now ruled in favor of the Bipartisan Campaign Finance Reform Act. Huge soft money contributions and barely disguised campaign commercials paid for by unregulated funds will no longer be the rule in our politics. Yet no one is under the illusion that such modest reforms will fundamentally reduce the influence of money in our politics. New mechanisms are already being created to circumvent the new rules, and as long as candidates need large sums of money to run campaigns and get their message out to voters, private large-scale financial backers will find ways to flow the money in, and elected officials will still be overly responsive to them.

However, the court also clearly said that the state has a powerful interest in preventing corruption and the appearance of corruption in our election processes. The challenge is to continue to move forward, to build systems of public financing that allow all candidates the opportunities afforded now only to wealthy candidates or those who succeed at the relentless fundraising grind that contemporary politics has become. This important reform has gathered significant steam. In Maine and Arizona, there have been two election cycles conducted under the new rules of "Clean Money" public financing. In both those states, increasing numbers of candidates use the system, and invariably they say that it has liberated them and allowed them to spend their time meeting voters and attending community events, rather than dialing for dollars. In New York City, a strong four-to-one matching system for candidates for municipal office encouraged an unprecedented variety of candidates to run and win in City Council races. In North Carolina and Wisconsin, efforts have succeeded in creating public funding systems for judicial elections, where the frightening relationship of campaign contributions and judicial decision-making is particularly stark.

Comprehensive campaign finance reform is a long-range effort. It is a difficult reform to win since it challenges the comfortable status quo. Even in those places where it is won, opposition often from key political leaders who liked the old system just fine, can undermine the reforms, as happened in Massachusetts. But the need to disentangle our politics from big money is essential, if people are to believe that their investment in the political process is worthwhile.

OTHER REFORMS: LET MANY FLOWERS BLOOM

These four reforms by no means exhaust the list of policies that states could adopt that would increase participation and make our democracy work in a more lively, vibrant, and inclusive way. Different states have different histories and issues, and reform advocates have many efforts on their radar screens. The list is long, but some bear at least a mention here:

- Adopting and expanding mail-in voting based on the positive experience of Oregon and Washington, without eliminating Election Day voting and registration activities.

- Making Election Day a holiday, as most European countries do. Making working people vote only on one, working day makes it difficult to find the time while creating lines and delays at particular points of the day.

- Allowing full representation in Congress for residents of Washington, DC.

- Allowing sixteen- and seventeen-year-olds to pre-register to vote while in high school as a corollary to expanding civic education.

- Dropping restrictive requirements on who can vote by absentee ballot.

- Allowing voting by noncitizens where not constitutionally prohibited, for instance in school elections, where children of new immigrants are deeply affected by the decisions but have no voice in their formulation.

The list could go on even further; the magnitude of the task of restoring our democracy, and earning people's trust in it, is huge. Progressives need to seize this moment and take the lead in these issues. Morally, the progressive ideals of equality and justice can never be attained if vulnerable segments of the population—young people, low-income communities, and people of color—continue to be pushed out of the political process, and if the wealthy can dominate our political processes with financial power. In addition, it is to the advantage of conservatives to have a narrow, distorted, and bleached electorate. To the degree that America's electorate truly reflects America's breadth and diversity, then the needs and aspirations of that true majority will become the focus and the direction of our democracy and our politics. If that isn't worth working on, it's hard to say what is.

Chapter 13
The Lessons of Paul Wellstone

Many of us mourn the loss of Paul and Sheila Wellstone, and feel the absence of their energy, purpose, and passion. Paul demonstrated the potential for a leader who is prepared to stand up for what he believes, and for a progressive who is prepared to counter money politics with people politics. Here, Jeff Blodgett, his friend, campaign manager, and now director of Wellstone Action, describes just how he did it.

The Winning Ways of Paul Wellstone
by Jeff Blodgett

IT IS SOMEHOW FITTING that the anniversary of Paul Wellstone's death will always fall near election day. When his plane went down, he was twelve days from winning a very difficult race for a third term in the U.S. Senate. What a victory it would have been. Wellstone was bucking all the trends in 2002. He was an outspoken progressive, running against the hand-picked candidate of Karl Rove and the Bush White House. He was winning in a year when Democrats were pounded across the country. He boldly stood up for what he believed in a year when Democrats struggled to find their voice. He mobilized hundreds of thousands of people through his campaign organization in a year when Republicans did better than Democrats on the ground in many states.

Winning tough, statewide elections is part of Paul Wellstone's legacy. He succeeded in politics because he drew heavily from his days as a community organizer, combining ongoing organizing with large-scale grassroots electoral work. All the while, he was pushing a bold progressive agenda in the United States Senate. Wellstone provides a model for progressives who are serious about winning in the future. (And it won't just be once a year that the Wellstone approach is remembered. It now lives on through the Camp Wellstone political training program coming to a city near you in 2004 and beyond.)

How did Paul win elections, even in the toughest of political environments? There are at least three factors that contributed including:

Harnessing the power of a highly energized base. Wellstone invested seriously in his field organization, and his highly proficient grassroots campaigns turned him into a progressive who could win. His campaigns were run and won on the notion that you first energize a large base and connect deep down in communities, then turn that support into a working organization as you go out and move enough undecided voters to win an election. Wellstone figured out the ways to engage huge numbers of people to propel his campaigns (17,000 active volunteers in 2002). This army of volunteers moved undecided voters in Paul's direction with multiple direct contacts at the doorstep and on the phone. In addition to the worker, environmental, and other liberal constituencies, his base went very deep with more disenfranchised groups like youth, immigrant communities, and communities of color. Many give lip service to this way of campaigning, but few do it right.

Close connection to communities. At his core, Paul Wellstone was a community organizer, having spent decades working on civil rights and poor people's movements. His background doing rural populist organizing gave him an appreciation of the mutual power that is built when leaders stay engaged and grounded in people, communities, and their organizations. As senator, he spent as much time helping organizing efforts as he did legislating, and understood the direct linkages between the two. Wellstone believed that part of his job was to draw attention to the good work of his allies. He lent his time and energy to union organizing drives, ran strategy sessions with mental health advocacy groups, helped families connected through afflictions like Parkinson's and MS to organize themselves into a force. He helped nurture long-term organizing and activism that did not come and go with election cycles but in the end helped him win elections and be an effective U.S. senator.

Winning votes with the courage of conviction. Paul Wellstone pushed a bold progressive agenda as senator, all the while maintaining majority support in his state. A big reason was that Minnesotans awarded him for his authenticity. He was clear about where he stood and for what he believed, and then he let the chips fall as they would. It turned out that some voters prefer elected officials who speak their minds than ones they agree with on every issue. And for his base, Wellstone's conviction politics elicited the passion and excitement that fueled his campaign organization. The best illustration of this was Wellstone's vote against Bush's Iraq war, one month before the 2002 election. But there are other examples such as his vote against Clinton's welfare reform bill late in the 1996 reelection campaign, or his being only one of three in the U.S. Senate to vote against aid to Colombia. Progressives will do better when our candidates and leaders understand that communicating and acting on what you believe in can often be more important than the position itself.

These three elements—grassroots campaigns, supporting community organizing, and progressive leaders operating with conviction—is the Wellstone way. It's also a model that can be applied by others.

This is where the Camp Wellstone political training program comes in. The idea is to blend together the concepts of community organizing, large-scale grassroots campaigns and progressive leadership, along with intensive training in the nuts and bolts of effective political work. The weekend-long session, put on by Wellstone Action, the nonprofit, nonpartisan group set up by sons Mark and David Wellstone, runs in three tracks: working on a campaign; organizing and activism; and being a candidate. This three-track strategy reflects the Wellstone belief that people working on electoral campaigns and community organizers can learn much from each other. In addition, you need candidates and office-holders who practice a style of leadership and campaigning that enhances community-building and broadens the base for larger change.

Camp Wellstone travels to cities where this kind of organizing can make a difference. Wellstone Action will team up with like-minded organizations to put on several camps a month in key states in 2004 and beyond. The camps will help thousands of people around the country hone their political skills, run good campaigns in their communities, build stronger organizations and run confidently for office.

Paul Wellstone wrote in his book, *Conscience of a Liberal* about the critical ingredients for effective political activism: "Good ideas and public policy, so that your activism has direction; grassroots organizing, so that there is a constituency to fight for the change; and electoral politics, since it is one of the ways people feel most comfortable deciding about power in our country." Wellstone practiced what he preached, and ended up making a difference in the lives of many by building progressive power. Above all, Paul Wellstone would want others to keep learning how to help make the progressive movement more capable, strategic and successful. The best tributes to Wellstone will not come at the end of October every year, but every time progressives embrace his legacy of organizing, advocacy, and winning elections.

DOONESBURY © 2002 G. B. Trudeau. Reprinted with permission of UNIVERSAL PRESS SYNDICATE. All rights reserved.

CHAPTER 14
Taking Back the Media

In an era when the influence of corporations on government decision-making rivals the power of the trusts in the Gilded Age, something remarkable is taking place: a democratic movement against media consolidation. As John Nichols and Robert McChesney argue below, progressives must now not only challenge the increasing concentration of ownership in the media and work to expose how it is undermining democracy by placing more and more broadcast and cable outlets, radio stations, newspapers and Internet sites into the hands of companies guided only by commercial and bottom-line values but they must also lay out an agenda for a media reform movement that is sustainable enough, broad-based enough and powerful enough to forge real changes in ownership patterns, and in the character and content of American media. Not only should progressives make media reform part of the 2004 Presidential debate and all the campaigns that follow it, but they should make it part of the kitchen-table debates where the real course of America can, and should be, plotted. If the initial challenge was one of perception making media democracy and reform an issue the next challenge is one of organization.

Up in Flames[*]
by Robert W. McChesney and John Nichols

POOR, POOR, PITIFUL MICHAEL POWELL. His term as chairman
of the Federal Communications Commission was supposed to
be easy. He thought that like FCC chairs before him, his job was
to jet around the country meeting at swank resorts with the
CEOs of major media companies, take some notes, and then
quietly implement their sweeping agenda for loosening the last
significant constraints on media consolidation in the United
States. Nobody except some corporate lobbyists and their political acolytes would know what was going on. Then, when his
term was up, he would get a cushy job with industry or another
plum political appointment. Look at his predecessor, William
Kennard, who now rakes in big money brokering telecommunications deals for the Carlyle Group. It was supposed to be a win-
win scenario for Powell and the people he regulated.

Instead, everything went wrong. The FCC broke its traditional lockstep and experienced a very public 3-to-2 split in
June 2003 votes that narrowly endorsed six media-ownership
rule changes, including one that would allow a single network to control television stations reaching 45 percent of all
American households and another that would allow one
media company to buy up the daily newspaper, as many as
three television stations, eight radio stations, and (thanks to
a separate court ruling) the cable system in a single market.
Then, despite the fact that Powell claimed he was acting

* From *The Nation,* November 17, 2003

under pressure from the judiciary, a federal appeals court blocked the changes until a full judicial review could determine whether the public interest was being damaged. A few days later, while Powell continued to insist he was relaxing the rules to meet the congressional mandate contained in the Telecommunications Act of 1996, the Senate voted overwhelmingly to block implementation of the changes. By the end of the year, all of Powell's rationales had blown up in his face like a trick cigar.

And things could be getting worse for Powell. Even as the Bush White House seeks to preserve the FCC chair's handiwork—presumably on the theory that it is payback time for big media companies, like Clear Channel, General Electric, and Rupert Murdoch's News Corporation, that have supported Bush's campaigns—the conservative leadership in the House is faced with an unprecedented revolt among Republicans, who are signing on to a bipartisan letter that demands a vote on whether the chamber should join the Senate in disapproving the rule changes.

Powell purports to know why things have gone awry. In a remarkable series of interviews with the *New York Times*, the *Washington Post*, and CNBC, Powell said the normal rule-making process had been upset by "a concerted grassroots effort to attack the commission from the outside in." Seemingly unaware that a public agency like the FCC could, in fact, be addressed by the public, he expressed amazement that as many as three million Americans have contacted the FCC and Congress to demand that controls against media monopoly be kept in place. Capitol Hill observers say media ownership has been the second most discussed issue by constituents in 2003, trailing only the war on Iraq. Following Brecht's famous dictum, Michael Powell wants to fire the people.

Who are these attackers of the status quo who have so upset Powell's best-laid plans? Noam Chomsky and William Safire both came out against the rule changes. So did Common Cause and the National Rifle Association. Reformer Gene Kimmelman of the Consumers Union and conservative Brent Bozell of the Parents Television Council cowrote an op-ed opposing Powell's rules relaxation. People who disagree on just about everything found themselves in agreement that in this debate over whether a handful of corporations should be allowed to dominate the discourse—the already fragile health of American democracy was at stake.

Powell's attempt to co-opt this anger by organizing public hearings on insuring local content on radio and TV failed miserably. The first hearing, on October 22, 2003, in Charlotte, North Carolina, drew an overflow crowd that cheered songwriter Tift Merritt when she told Powell, "To try to talk about localism without discussing media ownership is avoiding the issue." Independent Rep. Bernie Sanders of Vermont, the leading congressional critic of media monopoly, explains that, "It is not a coincidence that everything blew up the way it did this year. The American people know they are getting less information than they had before about decisions that are being made in their name, and they know that we are passing some critical points where, if we don't act, citizens are not going to have the information they need to function in a democracy."

The diversity of the opposition confirms that the FCC rules have become a lightning rod for concerns not just about the specific issue of consolidation of media but also about a host of systemic flaws that have become evident as mass media have come increasingly to be defined by commercial and corporate concerns. People who have long felt shut out of the mainstream of American media—people of color, women, trade unionists, and farmers—stood with families concerned about excessive violence and sexuality on television and in the movies. Journalists who found it harder and harder to do their job for reasons ranging from staffing cuts to inappropriate pressure to appear patriotic found common ground with activists still furious over the collapse of serious coverage of the 2000 election in general and the Florida recount fiasco. They were joined by masses of citizens who had watched with increasing disgust after September 11 as supine reporters unquestioningly accepted administration contentions regarding the terrorist attacks and the Afghanistan and Iraq wars that followed.

Americans recognize that their media are experiencing digital Wal-Martization. Like the chain that earns billions but cannot be bothered to pay employee health benefits, major media concerns in the United States brag about their profits to Wall Street but still cry poor when it comes to covering the news that matters to Main Street. A 2002 study by the Project on the State of the American Newspaper found that the number of reporters covering state capitals across the country full-time had fallen to just over 500, a figure the *American Journalism Review* described as "the lowest number we have seen, and probably the lowest in at least the last quarter century." Is this the market at work? Have citizens demanded, in the midst of a period of devolution that has made state governments more powerful than ever, that they get less state capitol coverage? Not at all. "It comes almost entirely as a consequence of newsroom budget cuts by companies seeking to bolster their shrinking profit margins during an economic downturn," says *AJR*. Those cuts parallel a decline in political coverage on television news programs, which fell in 2002 to the lowest level in decades. And what if one corporation owned the newspaper as well as TV and radio stations in the same market? "It's a given that you'll see more cuts in staffing, fewer reporters covering city halls, state capitals, Washington and the world," says Newspaper Guild president Linda Foley. "And people know that. They know that if one company owns most of the media outlets—in their town, in their state, or in the country as a whole—they are going to get a one-size-fits-all news that is a lot more likely to serve the people in power than it is the public interest and democracy."

To many Americans, it seems clear that the one-size-fits-all moment has already arrived. After years of decreasing international coverage—all the major television networks have shuttered foreign bureaus over the past decade in a wave of cutbacks that Pew International Journalism Program director John Schidlovsky refers to as "perhaps the single most negative development in journalism in my lifetime"— the United States found itself in March on the verge of launching a major invasion of a Middle Eastern country that most Americans could not locate on a map.

Indeed, it was the war on Iraq that triggered some of the most intense opposition to Powell's rules changes. At Bush's last prewar press conference, the White House press corps looked more like stenographers than journalists. Even some reporters were appalled; ABC News White House correspondent Terry Moran said the reporters looked "like zombies," while Copley News Service Washington correspondent George Condon Jr. told *AJR* that it "just became an article of faith among a lot of people: 'Look at this White House press corps; it's just abdicated all responsibility.'" Millions of Americans agreed. "I talked to people everywhere I went who said that if the media, especially the television media, had done its job, there wouldn't have been a war," says Rep. Jim McDermott.

Powell only poured gasoline on the flames when he declared that the "thrilling" TV coverage of the war proved there was nothing to be concerned about with regard to media consolidation. Antiwar groups like MoveOn.org and Code Pink, which did not share Powell's view, became prime movers in the burgeoning movement to block the rules changes, providing vehicles for communicating grassroots sentiment to the FCC and Congress via MoveOn's networks and organizing protests and petition drives across the country.

But Powell's problems involved far more than antiwar activism. Even inside the guarded palace that houses the FCC in Washington, the chairman faced opposition. Concerned that the rules changes threatened the public interest he was sworn to uphold, dissident FCC commissioner Michael Copps organized more than a dozen informal hearings around the country where academics, journalists, musicians, and others spoke in virtual unanimity against the changes. Another FCC member, Jonathan Adelstein, often accompanied Copps. He, too, heard that rather than relaxation of the ownership rules, most people wanted them tightened. Copps and Adelstein went on to cast the two June 2003 votes against the changes. For his part,

Powell refused to attend the hearings, claiming he was too busy. (Powell was indeed busy: The Center for Public Integrity revealed that the chairman, the two other GOP commissioners, and their aides held dozens of closed-doors meetings with corporate lobbyists and CEOs.)

Another galvanizing force in the fight over the rule changes was the growing awareness of the damage done by the relaxation of radio ownership rules in 1996: Radio quickly came to be dominated by behemoths like the 1,200-station Clear Channel and the 272-station Cumulus Media. Musicians like Don Henley told Congress about what a disaster consolidated radio had been for popular music. And in town after town when Copps held his hearings, the standard complaint was about the elimination of local radio news, or local programming in any form. This issue struck a chord not just with liberal activists but also with conservatives, who dislike the lack of local ownership and content that come with media concentration. Conservatives also maintained that the level of vulgarity and obscenity in popular culture was being driven upward primarily by the media conglomerates. By the end of the summer, Trent Lott and Jesse Helms joined Bernie Sanders and Rep. Barbara Lee in calling for overturning Powell's ownership-rules changes.

The strange-bedfellow coalitions that have developed are remarkable. But they have not yet been sufficient to win the fight. Though more than 200 Democratic and Republican members of the House signed a letter calling for a vote to overturn the FCC rules changes, that initiative was stalled by Speaker Dennis Hastert and majority leader Tom DeLay. MoveOn.org, Free Press, and other media reform groups conducted a major grassroots campaign to win enough signers to reach the "magic" 218 threshold that signals a majority of the House wants a vote—which could have pushed leaders to let the House voice its disapproval. The Bush White House did everything in its power to prevent that from happening, because if the overturn proposal passed, Bush's loyalty to the big media lobby would have put him under pressure to use what would have been his first veto to block a measure that is enormously popular. With his sliding poll numbers, such a veto would have played directly into the growing belief that Bush is an opportunist more concerned with aiding the bank accounts of his billionaire benefactors than representing the interests of the American majority.

Even if Bush could be forced to allow the rules to be overturned, a victory only locks in the rules that were in place on June 2, 2003. Indeed, as commissioner Copps notes, the changes represent "only the latest, although perhaps most radical step in a twenty-year history of weakening public-interest protections." Thus, win or lose, the great media reform fight of 2003 was less about reform than about preventing a corrupted, corporation-dominated status quo from growing even more corrupt and corporate.

It is important to win the fight against the FCC rule changes for both symbolic and practical reasons. But it is even more important to recognize that this is merely the beginning of a struggle for real media reform in America. That was the message of the first National Conference on Media Reform, which was attended by more than 1,800 activists on November 7–9, 2003, in Madison, Wisconsin, the focus will be on the future. "If all we do is fight defensive battles, the best we'll ever be able to hope for is that things won't get any worse. But that's not enough," says Sanders. "What we need is an agenda to make things better."

What are the pieces of that agenda?

- Rep. John Conyers, the ranking Democrat on the House Judiciary Committee, is right to argue for a renewed look at antitrust initiatives. Competition and diversity have been under assault for more than two decades, and it is time to consider the effect on the marketplace of ideas when reviewing media mergers. It is time, as well, for the federal government to engage in a period of study and debate leading to agreed-on caps on media ownership that are considered appropriate for a democracy. The current system of case-by-case review of proposed mergers, which frequently results in the making of exceptions for individual firms and then whole sectors of media, is an abject failure.

- Congress should roll back the number of radio stations a single firm can own. Sen. Russ Feingold is considering sponsoring such legislation. Congress should also be pushed to pass legislation prohibiting media cross-ownership and vertical integration. There are tremendous economic benefits to media conglomeration—but they accrue almost entirely to the media owners. The public gets the shaft.

- The regulatory process, which is in disarray and awash in corruption, must be reinvigorated. Commissioner

Copps will hold a series of town meetings this fall designed to draw attention to the power that citizens still have to challenge the licenses of local broadcast outlets. "Most people do not even know that they can challenge the renewal of a local radio or television station if they believe that the station is not living up to its obligation due to a lack of local coverage, a lack of diversity, excessive indecency, and violence, or for other concerns important to the community," says Copps. Activism needs to be directed at the hometown level, where broadcast licenses can be challenged.

• The promised expansion of access by not-for-profit groups to low-power FM radio-station licenses, which was scuttled by a backroom deal in Congress several years ago, must take place. Parallel to this shift in policy, tax incentives should be created to aid in the development of new, community-based, non-commercial broadcasting outlets.

• Funding for public broadcasting must expand dramatically. Only about 15 percent of funding for public radio and television comes from federal subsidies. And what funding does come from Congress is subject to great political pressures. Public broadcasting at the federal and state levels has the potential to provide a model of quality journalism and diversified cultural programming. But that won't happen if cash-starved PBS and NPR outlets are required, as some propose, to rely on the same sort of thirty-second spot advertising that dominates commercial broadcasting.

- Broadcasters must be forced to give candidates free air time. Senators John McCain and Russell Feingold, the authors of the only meaningful campaign-finance-reform legislation of the past decade, are now proposing such a requirement. Their initiative is essential to making not just better campaigns but better media. Currently, media conglomerates are among the most powerful lobbyists against both campaign finance reform and media reform. The system works for them, even as it fails the rest of us.

- Media conglomerates must not be allowed to impose their will on the United States and other countries via international trade deals. Media firms are currently lobbying the World Trade Organization and other multilateral organizations to accept a system of trade sanctions against countries that subsidize public broadcasting, that limit foreign ownership of media systems or that establish local content standards designed to protect national and regional cultures. They want similar assaults on regulation inserted into the proposed Free Trade Area of the Americas. Rep. Sherrod Brown is right when he says Congress should not pass trade agreements that undermine the ability of Congress to aid public broadcasting and protect media diversity and competition.

- Beyond specific regulatory and trade fights, the media reform movement must address what ails existing media. Still top-heavy with white men from middle-class backgrounds, TV news departments and major newspapers remain in thrall to official sources. Additionally, their obsessive focus on crime coverage and celebrity trials leaves no room for covering the real issues that affect neighborhoods and whole classes of people. Coverage of communities of color, women, gays and lesbians, rural folks, and just about everyone else who doesn't live in a handful of ZIP codes in New York and Los Angeles is badly warped, and it creates badly warped attitudes in society. Those attitudes shape the public discourse and public policy. Thus, media reformers must support the struggle to expand access to the airwaves and to assure that independent and innovative journalists, writers, and filmmakers have the resources to create media that reflect all of America.

This agenda is already long. And it is just the beginning. We have not even broached all the policies that will affect the Internet, such as copyright and access. That it is possible for a growing number of Americans to imagine these sorts of reforms being implemented provides a measure of recent progress. At the start of 2003, the conventional wisdom was that media reform was a nonstarter as a political issue—because even some activists feared it was too abstract for people to sink their teeth into, because the corporate lobbies owned the politicians and regulators, and because, for obvious reasons, there was next to no coverage of media policy fights. Now, the world looks very different. Media reform clearly registers with millions across the political spectrum. The range of issues being put into play provides rare opportunities for the forces of civil society to win tangible victories. Even small victories can have big meaning, but they won't come easily. Michael Powell may be shell-shocked, but the people who have grown accustomed to running media policy in this country—the media conglomerates, their lobbyists, and those politicians they still manipulate like channel clickers—aren't going to give up without a fight.

There is real work to be done. For a media reform movement that is sustainable enough, broad-based enough, and powerful enough to forge real changes in media ownership patterns, and in the character of American media, it is essential to build upon the passionate base of activists who did so much to make media an issue in 2003. We have to make media policy part of the 2004 presidential debate and all the campaigns that will follow it. And we have to make it a part of the kitchen-table debates where the real course of America can, and should, be plotted. To do that, the media reform movement that captured the imagination of antiwar activists and others in 2003 must burrow just as deeply into labor, church, farm, and community groups, which are only beginning to recognize how their ideals and ambitions are being damaged. If the initial challenge was one of perception—making media an issue—the next challenge is one of organization. "Media reform has become an issue for millions of Americans," says Bernie Sanders. "Now, we've got to make media reform more than an issue. We have to make it a reality for all Americans."

CHAPTER 15
Devolve This!

═══════════

As Joel Rogers argues below, "devolve this" should be turned into a progressive rallying cry, not a conservative ploy. His piece is a compelling strategic manifesto laying out the elements of much-needed progressive strategy in the states. "Who controls state politics controls American politics," he argues, and the Right, which understands the truth of this axiom, has been working it for years to its advantage. Decades of devolution and divestment from national government have made the states even more important places of politics than at any time in the past half-century. Some of the most important fights and progressive reforms for affordable health care, education, environmental protection and clean politics are taking place beyond the beltway. Thus, while it is essential to defeat Bush, it is also essential to understand that the road to progressive renewal may run through the states.

TOWARD A PROGRESSIVE STRATEGY IN THE STATES
by Joel Rogers

WHO CONTROLS STATE POLITICS controls American politics. The Right understands the truth of this axiom, and has been working it for years to its advantage. Progressives generally have not. More through inattention than adversity, the Progressive movement has no particular political strategy for the states, even though decades of devolution and divestment from national government have made them more important places of politics today than at any time in the past half century.

Progressive slowness to develop a state strategy is in some ways understandable. State variation and competition has historically been the single most resilient barrier to American national democratic advance. The very idea of a progressive *state* strategy—as against determined focus on a more democratic national government able to surmount that barrier—may seem oxymoronic, or merely moronic. It's also true that state politics is boring, or at least not as compelling as other politics. This is especially so today, with the nation at war and facing, from our own government no less, the greatest internal threat to our democracy in our history; but the observation holds in safer times. And last but not least, most progressives mourn devolution, which has been coterminous with if not defined by the destruction of the New Deal democratic welfare state, the greatest domestic achievement of twentieth-century American liberalism. We are in a sort of collective denial that "the era of big government is over."

But whatever the reasons for our neglecting the states, good and bad, we need to get over them. We need a progressive strategy in the states, because not having one is now doing us two sorts of grievous harm.

One is that we're getting killed in the states in conventional politics, with results we are likely to feel for years to come. For the first time in a generation, a rightist GOP has recently gained the edge in total governors, legislative chambers, controlled legislatures, and legislative seats. And in states no less than nationally, the Right is clearer on its ends than are the Democrats, and infinitely more aggressive in casting even modest electoral victories in policy cement. We need to counter this.

Two is that we're blinding ourselves to a truly enormous political *opportunity* in the states, today the most natural site of progressive political advance. States are this because they offer a unique combination of great policy importance and workable scale, with relatively porous political systems that we could organize to our advantage. In at least some states, we already have close to the organization density (for example, among unions, community organizations, or local advocacy groups) to do this. Most generally, states are attractive because the same forces that have disabled progressives nationally—declining national institutions, rising inequality, the growing separateness of our experience as citizens—have plowed their political fields for us, practically inviting a progressive response. This invitation is only underscored by the states' current fiscal crisis, which invites fundamental rethinking about state taxes and current expenditures on economic development, an issue on which we have clear views. But even when the immediate crisis passes, states will be the places we can best learn what progressive politics should now look like in America, under material conditions unalterably different from their last great surge forward in the late 1960s and early 1970s. That will be a politics of socially minded production, not just redistribution; and states are where we can most easily organize that to work. They are where progressives can reconnect with electoral majorities, experiment with new policies to serve them, and govern from our values.

A more serious state strategy than we have today would draw inspiration from the original Progressives of a century ago—the folks who worked out at the state level many of the ideas that later informed the New Deal welfare state. We could do this today by deliberately fostering progressive policy experiment in several states, targeting a few where we already have density for political breakthroughs, and then surfacing the results of both into national political debate. Nor need this longer-term effort in the states distract us from more immediate national concerns. To take the most important right now—getting rid of George W. Bush—getting more capacity in the states would actually help achieve that end, while also providing some insurance against its failure.

This suggestion that progressives develop a more comprehensive and ambitious strategy for the states builds on organizing already going on there by progressive activists. They have shown through diverse policy reforms—from campaign finance to health insurance for the poor, enhanced worker rights to environmental standards—that we can do things of significance and good in the states that help people in need while increasing our own power. But this work—and the most seasoned state activists would be among the first to point this out—still falls well short of the scale and scope that is possible, and required for lasting effect.

What are now lacking are two things, ideally offered in combination. One is the equivalent of statewide progressive political machines, capable of competing across the range of elections relevant to gaining core legislative and executive power. Two is a broad state progressive program or platform that candidates from those machines can run, be identified by, and actually advance in office. The first is needed to institutionalize control of public power, not just jog it one way or another in serial issues or legislative campaigns. The second is needed to make progressives—as a community concerned with state issues, not just national and international ones—visible to the mass public. Doing both these things in at least some places, and the second in most—with coordination in our efforts across them—are the rudiments of a progressive political strategy for the states. That's what we now lack as a movement.

But is such a strategy worth pursuing? That depends entirely on the claims just made: that states really are serious sources of power, that they are marked both by rightist advance and opportunity for us, and that a state strategy can complement other progressive aims.

DO STATES REALLY MATTER?

Do states really matter? Do they have enough power to be worth fighting for? In a word, yes.

Our national constitutional design enumerates limited powers for national government and assumes plenary powers of states. That means that states—consistent with respect for individual rights, and respecting the supremacy of any contrary federal law—can pretty much do whatever they please. Around this design two centuries of accumulated political custom have also grown up, giving states a privileged role in implementing and enforcing much federal law.

The result is that states do by far the largest share of governing in America. They write most law and give content to even more through interpretation and administration. Most government that affects us in our everyday social roles—as workers, consumers, taxpayers, owners, and citizens—tends first or finally to run through states. Economic development, health care and abortion access, privacy rights, marriage and the family, wage standards, public safety, criminal justice, prisons, land use and zoning, air and water quality, education and training, consumer protection, transportation, energy use, corporate law, insurance, union security, gender equity and comparable worth, public recreation, housing standards and availability, sprawl, city life, libraries and other community public goods—this list could be extended—are among these things. All those named, in fact, are areas where states, as against feds, have the weight of *primary* responsibility for outcomes.

Devolution has given states yet additional powers and responsibilities. Over the past two decades, successive waves of "new federalism" have "block-granted" states money with few if any federal restrictions on its use. New national programs in education and training, housing, transportation, and economic development have been federalized from the start. And older ones, as in the environment, have become increasingly state led. All this has increased their standing relative to national government.

Government spending numbers tell this story. In the 1950s the federal and state government share of GDP was roughly equivalent. Now states are bigger, very much bigger, in most ordinary government operations. Entering the new millennium, the federal government was basically a gigantic military operation, a couple of large insurance programs for old people, and a privileged manager of money, credit, and debt. By 2000—outside military spending, transfer payments, and debt service—its operation claimed only 2 percent of GDP. States, in contrast, claimed 10 percent. And this was before

Bush & Co. took a further wrecking ball to what was left of the nonmilitary nation state, and Grover Norquist declared his dream of shrinking it to bathtub size and taking us all back to the age of William McKinley—without unions, without significant business regulation of any kind, without a federal income tax—while keeping our vast military might.

Now to be sure, devolution has sometimes has saddled states with additional responsibilities without the means of achieving them. And sometimes "devolution" has simply been political code of "abandonment." The Right eviscerates some "affirmative" function of national government—that is, one that does something to protect workers and the poor from capitalism and the rich—and states are left to clean up the wreckage that follows. Urban policy is an example. Devastated central cities were effectively abandoned by the national government a generation ago. Without additional money, states were left on their own to deal with them ever since.

And then there are admixtures of such abandonment and more genuine devolution. Welfare reform is an example. That has both reduced assistance to the poor and fundamentally changed the content of that assistance, with the change in content largely driven by the states themselves in their discretionary use of federal monies. All this amounts to a very mixed bag of policy responsibility and resources. It also underscores the importance—as state variation in welfare reform underscores—of being in the game as they carry additional responsibilities and discretionary power. What seems beyond question is that, powerfully complementing their traditional powers, devolution has underscored states as the primary site of American government today. Nor does it show any sign of reversal.

But even if none of this impresses, consider finally that states are also arbiters of the most fundamental transaction in democratic politics—the electoral gain and transfer of power. States control elections, all elections, more or less from top to bottom. They set the rules by which public power is acquired. It is state legislatures, not the constitution, that give us our "winner takes all" election system and its resulting two-party duopoly. It is states that determine the boundaries of all election districts, including Congressional ones, which heavily determine which party will occupy them. It is also states that—through their determination of voting access, election schedules, and voter eligibility—make nearly all decisions about the marginal size and shape of the active electorate. And it is state electorates, never some elusive national one, that decide *all* U.S. elections. This includes the single national one we have, for president, who is (usually) chosen by an Electoral College consisting of discrete state delegations. And even here state legislatures have a further decisive role, since they determine whether or not those delegations will be proportional to their popular vote. Control of state government thus allows control of the size and shape of the electorate, the parties competing for its vote, and the accuracy of that vote's representation in both national government and at home. So far as democratic fundamentals go, it's hard to get more basic.

For those still only concerned with national politics, Tom DeLay's recent shenanigans in the Texas legislature may help bring the importance of these powers into focus. In the 2002 off-year elections, for the first time since 1870, the Texas House went Republican—only by a few seats, but enough for DeLay to spring into action, masterminding a Texas GOP reopening of the legislature's decennial redistricting of state congressional boundaries. Along with the low comedy of Democrats holding up in out-of-state motel rooms, what ensued produced a result of spectacular, if underreported, national significance. The redrawn districts are virtually certain to increase by six the number of House Republicans. And that in turn, given the already sclerotic nature of congressional competition, is virtually certain to assure Republican domination of the House through the end of the decade, if not beyond. (In 2002, only four House incumbents lost their seats, and under a tenth of races were decided by less than 10 percent of the vote.) Nor, certainly, is DeLay's example lost on his colleagues. Even less remarked but similar redistricting has gone on already in other big-ticket Republican controlled legislatures, such as Florida, Michigan, Ohio, and Pennsylvania. Even for the most nationally inclined, this is why having power in the states matters. Because it gives you power over Congress.

But point made. States are important.

THE TIPPING POINT

About thirty years ago, the Republican Right decided to take over the states, an effort understood as a natural "cut the tree and catch the fruit" complement to national devolution. They have substantially succeeded. In the early 1970s, when this determined effort began, Democrats were in nearly full command of state government. Along with thirty-two governors, they held fully 70 percent of all state legislative seats, and controlled thirty-seven legislatures.

In a state version of the story that is now familiar nation-ally, corporations and the cultural right made peace long enough for this holy war. They invested heavily in GOP state organization, made more explicit and operational a variety of ties between national corporate interests and state parties, and built a slew of supporting institutions to funnel money to emerging state Republican leaders, and spoonfeed them reactionary programs to push.

Thirty years later, the results are in. Republicans now have more governors (R28–D22), more legislative chambers (R53–D45), more controlled legislatures (R21–D17), and more partisan legislative seats (R3684–D3626). All bets are for this advantage to grow in coming years, as the South turns steadily more Republican, and the nation GOP continues to target vulnerable Democratic governors (next up, by GOP con-sensus, those in Missouri, Washington, and West Virginia).

What Republicans are doing with these small majorities is broadly familiar. Along with the redistricting scams already mentioned, they are constitutionalizing restrictions on state spending (as Governor Schwarzenegger recently proposed in California), cutting social services of all kinds, acting hostile to labor, privatizing an ever wider range of state functions, holding the line of punitive criminal justice, rolling back pri-vacy rights to the benefit of banks and insurance companies, avoiding the health insurance crisis, limiting medical and products liability, freezing state minimum wages, limiting consumer protections, cutting funding to public schools, dolloping out ever more expansive tax breaks to business, and playing the red meat game (gay marriage, concealed weapons, etc.). No surprises here. And so, if such Republican leadership continues to gain in the states, we can expect broadly more of the same. States will become more perfect pictures of inequality, market governance, and business cronyism. We'll all look a little more like Texas, and a little less like the America we remember, or hope some day to live in.

Call this the threat. It exists, it is growing.

But now let's complicate this picture.

First there are contrary electoral trends—or at least, in this darkness, some big points of light. For example, the same election in 2002 that saw, for the first time in fifty years, Republicans edge past Democrats in their share of partisan seats also saw the new election of a slew of moderately to very progressive Democrats. The same election in 2003 that saw that Republican lead widen also saw the Democrats retake the New Jersey state legislature, an important validation of the progressive environmental policies of Democratic governor Jim McGreevey, elected in 2001. To be sure, McGreevey now excepted, many of these new governors are frustrated by Republican-controlled or -dominated legislatures, and most spent their first year in a sort of fiscal hell, cutting programs to their base. If nothing else, however, their election shows that the public is receptive to a more progressive message than "all business all the time" Republican bromides. They also provide a natural audience for progressive message and program, if we have one to offer.

Second, and all important, what most impresses about state politics right now is how competitive it is. Not at the level of individual legislative elections, surely, where about 40 percent still go uncontested. Nor even in all states. But over the state system as a whole. The split in governors, chambers, and legislative control are all close enough that a single election or two could easily swing the parties back to parity. And the bottom line split on total legislative seats is already there. The difference in partisan share is a razor thin .7 percent—a number that might suggest competitiveness to anyone. Now is not the time for progressives to hunker down before inevitably Republican advance, but to figure out how to challenge it.

Third, there is the accumulating evidence that progressives—usually operating with extremely scarce resources, and without a political machine of their own—can make serious progressive policy inroads in the states. This work is too extensive and varied to be easily summarized. It includes clean money campaign finance rules; disclosure and claw-back rules on corporate subsidies; standards and trans-parency in other economic development assists; "smart growth" development policies encouraging dense develop-ment; the protection of open space; myriad health-care reforms, from pooled state purchase of drugs and insurance for the poor and uninsured to direct employer mandates of universal health care; paid family leave; changes in Unem-ployment Insurance and other worker benefit programs to cover temporary workers; first contract arbitration for workers not covered by the NLRA; "living wage" increases in the minimum wage above the federal level; apprentice-ship utilization standards on public construction projects, and bars on using public monies for union busting; "respon-sible employer" standards on state contracting; reclaimed community ownership of sports teams; tax-base sharing and other initiatives for regional governance and greater equity; wholesale redesign of state education and training systems to permit greater worker mobility, skills credentialing, and greater access to training; bans on factory farms; inclusionary zoning to break residential segregation; an endless stream of air and water quality initiatives, including multiple state efforts to meet or exceed Kyoto goals on greenhouse gas emissions, and dramatically increase state reliance on clean renewable energy sources; a breakthrough "minimum feasible reduction of greenhouse gases" state standard on vehicle emissions in the largest state car market (CA); and more. And this doesn't mention the even greater activity, below the state level. "Living wage" campaign successes in more than a hundred cities; "community benefits agreements" in local development projects; local rules to stop sprawl, keep out Big Box retail, promote energy efficiency, reclaim open spaces, widen transit options, reduce commute times, expand libraries, increase recreational options, improve teacher training, and in myriad other ways use government for its essential purpose (Madison): "the well being of the people."

So there is opportunity, too, and reason for hope. What's required now is smarter politics.

WHAT IT TAKES

What would it take to take better advantage of progressive opportunities in the states, to build on present organizing while bringing it to greater coherence and scale?

Essentially what's needed is a partial equivalent of what is already provided on the other side by the Right. As Paul Weyrich said at the time he founded ALEC (American Legislative Exchange Council), the funnel for much right-wing program and organizing in the states: "I look at what the enemy's doing and if they're winning I imitate it."

We need, in effect, an "ALEC for our side"—by which is meant not an imitation of that particular organization, but a series of supports to progressive electoral action in the states. In no particular order. . . . We need a clearinghouse on "best practice" model legislation and administrative practice, and all manner of supports to elected officials prepared to move them (talking points, examples of success elsewhere, expert support, and so on). We need a capacity to regularly convene progressive elected officials, both regionally and nationally, for program, leadership, and organizing training, and networking with each other and with nonelectoral progressive leadership, so that they get better and think of themselves as part of a movement. We need to maintain that network, and connection to the broader progressive movement, through regular communication and explicit coordination of efforts across different sites. We need to take care of progressive officials at election time, with money and other support. We need a well-equipped "war room" to provide targeted assistance in cases of special need in legislative or electoral fights—on-site expert help, campaign coordination, polling, opposition research, whatever it takes to win. And to broaden and tighten our ranks, we need a good program of candidate recruitment, training, and placement to take advantage of open and challengeable seats. In the vast sea of state elected officials, there are perhaps 300 or so who think of themselves as progressive. In addition to supporting them better, we need to vastly increase their ranks.

Getting this sort of infrastructure in place would not cost

much. Perhaps ten to fifteen million dollars a year for starters. A mere pittance, really, which shows how much of the work has already been done.

Note that we already have the talent and experience needed to do this work—the policy, campaign, training, and other organizing. Consider the program and achievements of community organization groups like ACORN (Association of Community Organizations for Reform Now), IAF (Industrial Areas Foundation), and Gamaliel; progressive central labor councils in literally dozens of cities, including Atlanta, Baltimore, Cleveland, Denver, Los Angeles, Milwaukee, New York, San Jose, San Diego, San Mateo, and Seattle; the myriad of local organizations working with them, as with LANNE (Los Angeleans Networking for a New Economy), in LA; networks of elected officials like the Western States Resource Center; Northeast Action; the many state policy groups now part of the EARN (Economic Analysis Research Network) network; the descendants of the old Citizen Action network now reassembled in U.S. Action; and such national providers of program and technical assistance as ALICE (American Legislative Initiative and Campaign Exchange), CAF (Campaign for America's Future), CBBP (Center on Budget and Policy Priorities), CPA (Center for Policy Alternatives), COWS (Center on Wisconsin Strategy), CLASP (Center for Law and Social Policy), Demos, EPI (Economic Policy Institute), EOI (Economic Opportunity Institute), GJF (Good Jobs First), IWPR (Institute for Women's Policy Research), NELP (National Employment Law Project), and Public Campaign. Our problem is less a lack of talent than its dispersion over so many different organizations, each with their own history and reason for being but together less than the sum of their parts. What is needed then is the glue to bring those pieces together, and scale up their capacity to the extent that they are prepared to collaborate toward the common aim of a progressive state strategy.

Note, too, that we already know where we want to go in state program. We want states to get on the "high road" of high-wage, low-waste, democratically accountable economic development, and close and get off the "low road" of race-to-the-bottom price competition; this treats people like road-kill, the earth like a sewer, and democracy as an unaffordable burden, rather than a powerful productive force in a well-run economy. Based on years of work, we even know what this "high road" looks like in its different parts—education and training, transportation and infra-structure, land use and energy, democratic reform and administration. We just need to connect the dots into a pic-ture, and show that more hopeful future to the public.

Note, finally, that we know this program would be pop-ular. We know this not just because it is clearly in the inter-ests of a vast majority of voters—high-roading business, labor, most people of color, most women, and the many res-idents of inner-ring suburbs, depressed rural communities, and central cities who are getting killed by present low-roading policy—but because our own organizing experience over the past decade or so has shown repeatedly that, given a choice, this is the choice that majority makes.

Which effectively addresses the last concern suggested above, on whether a state strategy might detract from achieving national progressive goals. Ask yourself: Would it be bad for progressives nationally to be identified in the states with a popular economic and social program, to greatly increase the number of elected officials loyal to us, and to forge a new majority political coalition that split the business community while uniting nearly everybody else? Would it even hurt in removing George Bush from office?

It's hard to see how.

CHAPTER 16
Win Back the Young

─────────

Danny Goldberg, one of the country's most socially active music business executives, laments the Democratic party's declining support among 18–24-year olds and argues that the Democrats need to run campaigns that are both politically savvy in conventional terms, but also passionate, idealistic and inclusive. Here, Goldberg, who co-produced MTV's first voter registration TV commercials in 1984, looks at some of the groups working this season to mobilize, energize and register young voters and lays out why it is so vital that in 2004 and beyond, Democrats find a moral and emotional framework for their message and candidate that appeals to both young and old voters.

YOUTH VOTE IN 2004
by Danny Goldberg

WHEN ASKED ABOUT HOW to get younger people to vote, Jehmu Green, executive director of Rock the Vote, an organization that works with musicians to engage youth in the political process, says simply, "If you ask them they will come." In light of the Democrats' dramatic decline from a 19-point margin ahead of Republicans among eighteen- to twenty-four-year-old voters in 1996, to no margin in 2000, many are wondering— Why haven't the Democrats asked better?

The reasons for this decline are both practical and psychological. On the practical side, Dan Glickman, former Secretary of Agriculture under Clinton, who currently chairs a program in public policy at the Kennedy School at Harvard, explains that, "Politicians avoid young people in part because they like predictability. They know that older people care about Social Security, they know that union members care about the minimum wage." This point is illustrated by the experience of the Young Democrats of Missouri, who have several hundred members in the St. Louis area. Joe Bruemmer, organizer of the group, has had little success in getting the attention of the party establishment is Missouri. "Democrats in my state act as if the younger generations do not have any interest in the future of this country, not to mention even talking about our issues. " He complains "that the primary Democratic message in the 2002 election was almost exclusively Social Security and prescription drugs, 'the Lipitor election.' "

A partial remedy to this problem is being developed by Seth Rosen, assistant to the vice president of the Communication Workers of America union. His post-2000/2002 election conclusion was, "this electorate sucks and we need a different one." Rosen and Oberlin professor Chris Howel are currently organizing a series of focus groups with young CWA members in Ohio and Michigan to determine what strategies Democratic politicians could employ to convert younger nonvoters to voters.

Socially conscious music-based organizations are also working to motivate young voters. Rock the Vote has collaborated with MTV to recruit 50,000 "street team" volunteers who will go to concerts and events and try to register young people to vote. Russell Simmons and the Reverend Ben Chavis have created the HipHop Summit that has registered thousands in each city where they have held an event. Both of these music business groups use rock and hip hop celebrities to add hipness to voting. TV producer and philanthropist Norman Lear has created Declare Yourself, a nonprofit organization that will distribute one million videos featuring animation by the creators of South Park and actors Vince Vaughn and Ben Stiller, urging kids to vote.

On another track, legislation is currently being proposed in California that would allow seventeen-year-olds to vote in primaries if they turned eighteen by the general election. However, logistics are not enough. Democrats need a better "vibe." Turning around the perception of condescension of actual antiyouth bias requires Democratic spokespeople and Washington insiders to change their tone, modify their message, and get rid of their subconscious hostility to younger people.

One example of this inherent hostility was revealed by Ann Gerhart of the *Washington Post,* who ridiculed actress Drew Barrymore when she appeared at a press conference for Lear's organization. Gerhart condescendingly wrote, "If only the actress would speak a comprehensible sentence." Well, Drew Barrymore, besides having maintained a successful acting career for more than two decades and producing several of her own movies including *Charlie's Angels,* can reach millions of people who will never read the *Washington Post.*

Even more toxic is the cynicism expressed by Candy Crowley of CNN, who sourly mocked the enthusiasm at a press conference that preceded the CNN/Rock the Vote debate, "Let me be the voice of wisdom. I remember seeing crowds of young people cheering for John McCain in South Carolina in 2000 and he got creamed in the primary."

Crowley is simply saying out loud the assumptions of most middle-aged Washington political insiders. Their theory is that the loud media noise made by young people is actually a distraction from the "real" work of getting older voters to the polls. What's amazing is that the certainty from such naysayers is balanced by a complete lack of rationality. Why would the Republican electorate of South Carolina, dominated by the influence of the likes of Pat Robertson, have any relevance for a national campaign for the Democratic nomination? Why is it assumed that appeals to younger people, in their own cultural language on issues that matter to them, would automatically have a negative effect on a campaign for older voters? Surely the art of majoritarian politics requires simultaneous messages to disparate groups.

Whatever else Howard Dean does or doesn't accomplish, he certainly got the joke that other Democrats, at first, did not. Dean's early popularity was commonly ascribed to his antiwar stance as if he were merely a surrogate for a vocal minority that had always been against Bush's war. But other candidates opposed the war more vehemently than Dean and yet garnered much more limited support. His accomplishment was an ability to appear "authentic" from the beginning, calling his campaign one for "the young and young at heart." Dean, who was a doctor before he entered politics, uses conversational language that seems more intimate and independent than the platitudes and niceties of conventional campaign rhetoric.

Those who lament the chronically low turnout from

younger people need only to notice the candidates who bucked the trend: Jesse Ventura, John McCain, Ralph Nader, Arnold Schwarzenegger, and Clinton in 1992.

In addition to their own self-interest, younger people want to associate what they think is good for the country and the world with their political choice. Conservatives have brilliantly framed all of their positions, even tax cuts, in the context of a moral worldview. For all of his maddening political agility, Clinton, at his best, conveyed a sense of determination to help provide better living conditions for the country as a whole. It is vital that Democrats find a moral and emotional framework for their political message and candidate, one that will appeal to both young and old voters.

Whoever opposes George W. Bush, they can be sure his team will be sophisticated about including young people in its target range. It is no coincidence that for many months in 2003, Bush was more popular among young people than older ones. His plainspoken language and his apparent moral indignation are superficially alluring. He will not be defeated simply by name-calling. The way to beat Bush is not to make fun of him for being a "cowboy," but to come across as a more progressive cowboy; not to make fun of his plainspoken style but to fight him in that very style.

Democrats who are scared by polls that show Bush being more popular with younger people than older people would be wise to learn from Iowa senator Tom Harkin. In 1984, before Rock the Vote was created, I produced the first voter registration spots for MTV. I asked Harkin, who was then a congressman running for his first Senate campaign, if he was nervous about the youth vote in light of the fact that polls showed Reagan to be very popular with younger people. "If I can't convince young people to vote for me I don't deserve to be elected," said Harkin who bucked the Republican trend in 1984 and has since been re-elected three times, always running campaigns that are both politically savvy in conventional terms, but also passionate, idealistic and inclusive.

SECTION VII

BUILDING TO WIN

Chapter 17
Building to Win

―――――――――

For the first time in decades, thanks in part to a fierce desire to beat Bush, progressives are coordinating, organizing, and building the independent capacity to drive their message, their values and their movement into the political debate and electoral arena. Katrina vanden Heuvel lays out the key elements in this emerging progressive infrastructure and argues that—no matter what happens in 2004—it is vital that these groups continue to build and work together after the election to develop long-term, coordinated goals within the progressive movement.

by Katrina vanden Heuvel

IT'S NOT HARD FOR progressives to see that we're in for the fight of our lives. George W. Bush has made it clear that mandate or no mandate, he will pursue an extremist far-right agenda. But, as Representative Jan Schakowsky insists, these are times to "organize, not agonize." Progressives have no choice but to fight back and build an America that is safer, healthier, better educated, more secure, and committed to shared prosperity and opportunity for all. But we must fight back in smart and coordinated ways. After all, the Right's success over the past generation, in defining our politics and its limits, comes in no small measure from its decades-long development of an imposing array of independent institutions, messengers, and media outlets. Now, for the first time in decades, thanks in part to a unifying and fierce desire to defeat Bush, progressives are coordinating, organizing, and building the independent capacity to drive their message, their values, and their movement into the political debate and the electoral arena.

We begin with an advantage. On fundamental questions, this administration and the Right are out of tune with the majority of Americans. Despite its apparent grip on contemporary politics, conservatism today is failing to meet the challenges facing the country: stagnation and global instability, inequality, corporate corruption, and unprecedented financial pressures on families. And in area after area, the majority prefers progressive alternatives to the failed policies of the conservative right. People are deeply skeptical of corporate abuse of power and are committed to a core set of values—fairness, equal opportunity, reward for hard work, and the responsibility of the powerful. Sure, the American people want us to govern from the center, but this isn't the center the Washington pundits and politicians talk about: Citizens want us to deal with issues that are at the center of their lives. They seek a politics that speaks to and includes them—affordable childcare and health care, quality public education, retirement security, a living wage, corporate accountability, environmental protection, clean elections and campaigns, and an internationalist foreign policy that will create real security. Furthermore, the leading causes of the civilizing movements of the past decades—civil rights, reproductive choice, environmental protection—have now entered the mainstream political discourse.

However, to effectively challenge the Right, progressives must have more than good ideas. As the late Senator Paul Wellstone used to say, if our whole is going to equal the sum of our parts, we need to build a powerful progressive infrastructure that can reach out to citizens with our values and ideas. We need to mobilize allies; identify, recruit, train and support the next generation of leaders, at both the local and national level; apply effective grassroots organizing to electoral politics; provide support for candidates while holding them accountable; run ballot initiatives (campaign finance, living wage, the right to organize); offer a vehicle for coordinated national and local issue campaigns; and galvanize a network of media-savvy groups with a broad-based message.

Of course, we need more resources, and more powerful and well-financed institutions. But, in many areas, we are already stronger on the ground than the Right, and while money is important, we've seen the impact of mobilization when people are energized and organized. Consider the antiwar movement that went from zero to 15 million in just a few months, with an explosion of activity in hundreds of towns and cities, culminating in a global march on February 15, 2003 leading even the *New York Times* to herald the growth of "the world's other superpower."

Or consider the coordinated actions—on the Net and in the streets—for global justice. These actions are magnified by the thousands of grassroots groups and labor-community coalitions who have been winning, across the country, on such issues as living wages, public financing of elections, banning sweatshop produced goods, and providing universal health care. Integrating the energy of these movements into our electoral capacity—not only for the crucial work of defeating Bush in 2004 but for the long term—is vital for making our whole equal the sum of our parts.

What would make up the different elements of a progressive infrastructure? Well, we already have key elements in place. But, we could do more to recruit and train people to take advantage of open and challengeable seats at the state and local level—building a "farm team" of progressive leaders. The growing number of organizations—already developing model legislation, providing support to candidates and movements through talking points, message development, program and legislative assistance, training and polling—need more support. We could also provide more effective coordination among national and state mass membership groups in crucial get-out-the-vote and registration efforts that would increase progressive clout in the electoral arena. We could integrate the new technologies for activism—online mobilization organizations such as MoveOn.org that could coordinate both on the Internet and in person, raising millions of dollars for candidates and causes in small contributions. Other models of creative citizen engagement are also bringing young people into the political process—building on the work of socially conscious music-based organizations like Rock the Vote and Russell Simmons's Hip-Hop Summit, which has registered thousands in the cities where it has held events.

Any doubt that we have the beginnings of this infrastructure was dispelled in June 2003 at the gathering of progressives convened by the Campaign for America's Future. More than 2000 participants from across the country—union activists, leaders of civil rights, women's, environmental, grassroots action, and religious groups, as well as leading public scholars and elected officials—joined to share ideas and strategy, and lay out core elements to challenge the destructive course of the self-described "movement conservatives" who now dominate Washington. The conference, according to the *Washington Post,* showed that "among Democrats, the energy seems to be on the left . . . there is a coming together of forces to try to resurrect the Democratic Party in the progressive realm." The conference not only energized the thousands who attended, but it was a powerful display of the creativity, energy, and will in the progressive community. And in providing a platform for progressive leadership and a forum for developing strategy for 2004 and beyond, CAF's gathering played a role similar to what the National Conservative Political Action Conference does so prominently for the Right.

The conference was also valuable for highlighting the work of a broad network of progressive organizations, activists, and leaders. CAF and the Center on Wisconsin Strategy, for example, used the conference to launch the Apollo Project—a bold policy initiative that unites the progressive base. Building on a newly formed labor-environmental coalition (the project is supported by seventeen unions and a broad cross-section of the environmental community), Apollo is designed to dramatically break our dependence on foreign oil by investing in energy-efficient and renewable technology, revitalizing America's industrial base, and creating millions of new jobs in energy efficient industries. (See Bracken Hendricks, "The Apollo Initiative.")

The ability to drive ideas like these—as well as our energy and values—into the national and state debates relies on strengthening organizations and think-tanks like CAF, which arm progressives with initiatives and issues, challenge conservative spin, educate Americans, and ensure that there is a progressive voice in the national debate. Washington, DC's newest progressive think tank, the Center for American Progress, is already well funded and promoting an aggressive Democratic message against Bush.

Organizations like the Economic Policy Institute, the Institute for Policy Studies, the Institute for America's Future, the Center for Budget and Policy Priorities, Public Citizen, and the Institute for Women's Policy Research operate on smaller budgets while providing an invaluable network for policy and message development. At the state and local level, the Economic Research Analysis Network—linking more than thirty state and national policy research centers—the Midwest Progressives Elected Officials Network, the Public Interest Research Groups—the descendants of the Citizen Action Network—now reassembled in US Action, the Center for Policy Alternatives, and the newest group on the scene, the American Legislative Issue Campaign Exchange, are working to counter the Right's powerful state organization—the American Legislative and Exchange Council. These groups, along with others, are developing coordinated policy and activist strategies, linking activists and legislators in campaigns for model legislation, exposing rightwing stealth agendas, and analyzing state budget issues. If better funded, this network could provide greater program support and message for a farm team of new progressive candidates and legislators—as well as setting up a "war room" to provide targeted assistance in cases of special need in legislative or electoral fights.

Building a bolder presence in the media is imperative if we're going to drive our ideas and values into the political debate. Although, with each passing day, our media landscape seems more FOXified and Clear Channelized, we're also seeing—for the first time—that media reform clearly registers with millions of people (see John Nichols and Robert McChesney, "Taking Back the Media"). That frustration with the rightward tilt of our media has fueled ambitious plans to build a progressive echo chamber in TV and radio, in columns and commentaries, and in the larger national debate, including developing a roster of progressive talk-show guests and pundits. Progress Media, for example, will launch a populist radio network this spring, with stations in at least five of the country's ten largest media markets. Its flagship program, *Central Air,* is designed to bring populist, late-night-TV sensibility to radio—tailored to appeal to people with MoveOn.org politics who crave Rush Limbaugh–style bite. (There are several other progressive radio networks in the planning stages.) Former Vice President Al Gore is in talks to launch a youth-oriented liberal cable network to counter the influence of Fox. Link TV, which broadcasts via satellite to more than 21 million US homes 24/7, is expanding. Free Speech TV currently reaches over 11 million U.S. homes. The fact that five of the country's top bestselling books in 2003 skewered the Right and Bush— including *Lies and the Lying Liars Who Tell Them,* by Al Franken, *Bushwhacked* by Molly Ivins, and *Big Lies* by Joe Conason— signals the resurgence of liberal ideas and humor in our skewed-to-the-right marketplace of ideas. Popular websites like BuzzFlash.com, Democrats.com, and TruthOut.com, as well as a growing number of weblogs, act as truth squads exposing the Administration's deceptions and holding right-wing politicians and pundits accountable. Web publications like TomPaine.com not only provide analysis and information but also get the progressive message out to a larger audience through "op-ads" in leading newspapers and magazines. Fenton Communications and the Center for American Progress, among other progressive outfits, are starting to train a network of progressive talk-show guests. And among progressive magazines, there is an unprecedented circulation growth and increase in website traffic—*The Nation*'s readership is now at an all-time high of 160,000, and *The American Prospect*'s is at 55,000—which attests to a new level of energy and engagement in the more traditional progressive media.

The power of the Internet to mobilize, engage, and raise funds for progressive causes and campaigns is another vital piece of the progressive infrastructure—and crucial for a new generation of activism. In the past year, MoveOn.org's savvy and pioneering work has brought millions into the streets and onto the net to oppose the war against Iraq and lobby the FCC against media consolidation. Its first "virtual" presidential primary was instrumental in putting Democratic presidential candidate Howard Dean on the map as an insurgent/outsider. MoveOn.org's work to hold our politicians and mainstream media accountable, its support of progressive campaigns, and its ability to raise astonishing amounts of money—in small donations—for anti-Bush ads and other good causes, is creating a new politics of fundraising—breaking the hold of Wall Street and big money on the money primary—and devising a new politics of citizen engagement. MoveOn.org is not alone in tapping the power of the net. Ben and Jerry's, Ben Cohen's TrueMajority.com, WorkingAssets.com and Meetup.com are others pioneering new web-based communications, fundraising, and activism.

In the electoral arena, there is a dawning recognition that the Right cannot be challenged with "kinder, gentler" variations on conservative themes. If Howard Dean's campaign for the Democratic nomination shows anything, it is that there's a hunger for an aggressive and impassioned progressive message. This goes far beyond the inner circles of the Democratic Party or the Left. Witness the victories of aggressive progressives—like North Dakota State Senator April Fairfield, a farm activist, who used populist economic positions as a touchstone for a campaign that in 2002 saw her win a district that two years before, voted overwhelmingly for Bush. And on the national landscape, progressive leaders, including Dick Durbin and Jon Corzine in the Senate and Jan Schakowsky and George Miller in the House, have launched independent efforts to take off the gloves, organize a truth squad and challenge the extremism and corruption of this administration. Backed by a coordinated message, aggressive communications strategies and targeted issue campaigns, they plan to generate the "echo effect" so vital to driving an argument through the filter of the media.

And among national progressive mass-membership groups working to defeat Bush, there is a degree of unity and coordination not seen in a generation. Confronted with this administration's unrelenting assault on progressive values, environmental, civil rights, women's, and labor groups are putting aside past organizational differences and focusing on the importance of building a united and distinct progressive presence in electoral politics. These groups are sharing voter and membership lists, and organizing well-coordinated and targeted get-out-the-vote (GOTV) and registration efforts. America Votes, America Coming Together (ACT), Moving America Forward, and Partnership for America's Families are the leading voter-outreach organizations (called 527s in the argot of election law) that have formed since the McCain-Feingold campaign-finance-reform law prohibited the national party committees from raising money to fund such efforts. America Votes—a coalition of twenty-four national progressive mass-membership groups—is developing GOTV operations in more than fifteen presidential battleground "swing" states. And for the first time, labor has a central place at the table with other mass membership organizations, sharing polling data, research, and mailing lists, and hammering out election strategies. Organizations involved range from the Sierra Club, Emily's List, the NAACP, ACORN, and People for the American Way to NARAL, the AFL-CIO, MoveOn, and US Action. America Votes will have help from the new political action committee, America Coming Together—which expects to raise close to $100 million by Election Day. The Media Fund, a $50 million media campaign to support the Democratic nominee, will work to complement ACT's ground war. Moving America Forward is focused on registering Latino voters. And the Partnership for America's Families, headed by former AFL-CIO political director Steve Rosenthal, is establishing field operations and registering and engaging African-Americans, Latinos and working women in some seventeen battleground states. And the AFL-CIO, which has already dramatically expanded the influence of union households on elections, is launching a new expansion of its program that will take its message to workers who are not part of any union.

The work of building a strong progressive infrastructure is one that will require not a year but a decade or more. After all, the strategy of moving from election to election, crisis to crisis, hasn't gotten progressives far in recent memory. That's one reason why Progressive Majority, the savvy operation under the direction of Gloria Totten, is such a promising political initiative. PM understands that not only must we find and cultivate fresh talent, we should support our team of progressive candidates while they run—with message, program, talking points, opposition research, and all the other tools that the right routinely provides for its own. PM and its newest political program, PROPAC, a new progressive political action committee—modeled on Newt Gingrich's GOPAC—the vehicle by which he rose from Congressional backbencher to House Speaker in fourteen carefully plotted years—are explicitly dedicated to working at the grassroots to develop lasting relationships to identify, recruit, train, and support candidates who champion a broad progressive economic and social agenda.

Progressive Majority's ambition is nothing less than to design a bold strategy to redefine progressive electoral politics by transforming Democratic Party candidate-recruitment programs. And its network of web-based small donors is already providing seed funds for progressive challengers in targeted races. In addition, the new Wellstone Action, a center formed by the late senator and his wife Sheila's family and friends, is organizing and training hundreds of organizers and activists to work in voter registration and mobilization projects, like those organized by America Coming Together and America Votes, and to help thousands hone their political skills, run good campaigns in their communities, build stronger organizations, and run confidently for office.

The obvious challenge is for these groups to continue to build and to work together after November 2004 to develop long-term, coordinated goals within the progressive movement. It would be a shame if this unprecedented unity were exhausted in this, admittedly critical, presidential race. Where we can do so without doing harm to the achievement of our short-term goals, we should be looking at down-ballot races and, most controversial and important, at how we propose to organize ourselves after November 2004. Shouldn't we start discussing, early in 2004, how we will handle nonpresidential politics this cycle, and how we will be coordinated as a movement after the election? It will be easier to do this now than in the heat of the final months of the presidential race.

No matter what happens in the election, it is vital to sustain our emerging progressive infrastructure after the election. The great unraveling—likely no matter who wins—will provide both great challenges and great opportunities for progressives—and it is essential that we continue to build and grow and be ready to lead.

The real test before us is whether we can take everything we're doing right and do it even better, do it more, and do it in a coordinated way with passion, confidence, purpose, and principle.

CHAPTER 18
Growing a Progressive Majority

Every presidential year focus naturally goes to the race for the White House. In 2004, the stakes seem particularly high. But building a progressive majority for reform will take far more than winning one election. Progressives have to build the independent institutional capacity for policy initiatives, message development, candidate recruitment and support. One of the more promising initiatives is Progressive Majority, a new political action group devoted to recruiting, supporting, and electing the next generation of Paul Wellstones. Here, its director, Gloria Totten, describes her strategy.

GROWING A PROGRESSIVE MAJORITY
by Gloria Totten

THE ECONOMY IS GROWING, but this country is still in crisis. We've gone from record surplus to record deficits at the federal level. Over 10 million workers are without jobs; over 43 million have no health insurance. Our soldiers are still fighting a war the president announced was over. The clock has been turned back on our civil and economic rights, and many of the environmental protections we've fought for are already gone.

Yet, George Bush isn't running scared. He has told his team, don't give me "a lonely victory." While Bush is out raising money, his staff is putting together a comprehensive campaign strategy that includes voter registration and mobilization—for Bush, for his allies in Congress, and for their new recruits. The Right has made it clear that they see 2004 as their opportunity to break the partisan parity that exists and finally achieve a lasting majority.

They believe this is possible because they have been working toward it for decades.

In the late-1970s, Democrats were in control. Jimmy Carter was president. Both chambers of Congress were held by the Democrats. There were only twelve Republican governors. Republicans controlled only eleven state legislatures. But there was a resurgence brewing on the Right thanks to a cadre of aggressive, young conservative leaders who were developing new strategies for seizing power. These early foot soldiers first worked outside the Republican Party structure—creating new tactics for mass mobilization and fund-raising, developing hundreds of media voices for radio and television, building independent candidate recruitment and support operations. They moved into government slowly as elected officials, aides and policy experts. Over time, they moved inside and took over the Republican Party.

All of this was achieved because the New Right recognized that trying to work solely through the Republican Party structure would not reap the rewards they could attain by building their own independent political effort. Therefore, they not only invested in strategies that would serve their short-term goals—they helped elect a president in 1980—but they built their movement for the long term.

New Right leaders understood that it would take a wide

array of tactics to accomplish their goals. They built ultra-conservative think tanks, such as the Heritage Foundation and the Free Congress Foundation, to develop policy and disseminate message. These organizations trained new spokespeople to take on liberals, armed activists with information they needed to flood the airwaves, and nurtured new organizers.

Groups like the Moral Majority, the Christian Coalition, and the Family Research Council ran massive voter registration and mobilization campaigns that helped hundreds of conservatives get elected knowing they owed their victory to conservative causes.

Conservative leaders and funders also determined that they needed to build their own farm team of movement conservatives if they were going to have enough candidates to realize their dream of being in the majority. A national coalition of independent PACs was led by the National Conservative Political Action Committee. In 1978, GOPAC was formed by Delaware's Republican governor Pete du Pont, who noted that the Republican Party did not have enough political leaders at the ready to challenge Democrats for office.

GOPAC began a serious candidate recruitment, training, and support program that caught fire after the election of Ronald Reagan in 1980. Newt Gingrich took over the organization in 1986 with the goal of using GOPAC as a vehicle to take over the Congress. Gingrich brought renewed focus and energy to GOPAC; he recruited and trained thousands of leaders who ran vibrant campaigns at the local, state, and federal levels. And in 1992, when Republicans took over Congress, Gingrich had a legion of candidates running on the same message and the same agenda.

The New Right made their gains because they made a concerted, intentional, and strategic political effort. They worked over years to see their vision become reality. They didn't just focus on one strategy, one race, one body of power. There were many organizations, leaders, and campaigns that worked in tandem to gain lasting control at many levels.

Now for the first time in decades, progressives have begun organizing with the level of cooperation and discipline that it will take to defeat the Right, and build a majority in American politics. There is a level of focus rarely seen on our side, thanks in part to our unified desire to defeat Bush and in part to progressive leadership that is willing to fight harder to win elections.

But why does it always seem to take a crisis for our organizations and constituencies to work together? Certainly, there's no easy answer to this question. Most definitely, establishing and implementing long-term and coordinated goals within our movement will help address this challenge.

Instead of moving from crisis to crisis, we ought to pause and think about whether or not we are implementing a cohesive strategy for our long-term gains—whether we are building our movement. The strategy of moving from state to state and from election to election hasn't gotten us far in recent memory. Today, conservative Republicans hold the presidency and both chambers of Congress, there are twenty-nine Republican governors, and Republicans control twenty-one state legislatures.

Movements have a hard time surviving when we empty our coffers to defeat an incumbent and are without a plan to capitalize on the victory or recover from the defeat. Are we making sure that when we turn a voter out to vote against Bush that there are other progressives on that ballot? Have we identified who will run for vulnerable congressional seats two elections from now—seats we can win if we begin building now? Are we investing the time our young leaders need to become serious politicians? Do we know where we need to win locally to affect redistricting in 2011? Thinking beyond the next election, the next ballot initiative, the next caucus and primary will help determine how progressives can serve the movement more effectively and efficiently.

That's why Progressive Majority recently launched PROPAC—the program through which we will recruit, train, and elect the next generation of leadership. We will work at the grassroots level with state partners to build a farm team of progressive candidates adequately prepared to run for election. Beginning in 2004 in five targeted battleground states, we will identify the strongest progressive leaders, recruit them to run for office, train them on how to campaign, raise money, and articulate a clear, compelling progressive message. We will deliver hard political campaign assistance; assist them with raising money to get their message out; and connect them to a broader network of elected officials, advocates and other candidates so they will be committed and well-connected officeholders. After 2004, we won't leave. We'll continue to work in those states to prepare for the next election, and the next. We'll target five additional states in 2006, and five more in 2008 until we've established candidate recruitment as part of the permanent political infrastructure in the top battleground states in the nation.

PROPAC will be an effective vehicle to recruit progressive leaders to public service because it goes beyond traditional programs to provide the political campaign support and pragmatic skills candidates need to win in today's political environment. Imagine how we will reengage voters when they see not one, but hundreds, of candidates effectively fighting for the issues they believe in.

For good reasons, everyone is focused on 2004. But progressives must have the discipline and maturity to build for the long-term. We must find ways to link short-term and long-term projects. We're building a movement to change the country, not simply win one election. With the country in crisis and the Right confident it is about to consolidate a governing coalition, there is no better time to begin.

REGIME CHANGE CAFÉ
HOT AND TASTY FARE FOR A HUNGRY PUBLIC

APPETIZERS

APOLLO ALLIANCE ANTIPASTO
Hope. Ambition. Smart Politics. We've got the right recipe—we just need to serve it up in more places. Ask about our Rust Belt specials.

BUSH POPULARITY DIP
When Bush and his surrogates sell their propaganda in cities and towns, we need to challenge them. Platter includes t-shirts, bumper stickers, and other spicy forms of guerilla media. Mime troupes not included. Bulk pricing available.

16 WORD SURPRISE
Support for speakers' bureau and college tours for Joe Wilson and other Administration critics. Priced by the mile.

SPECIALS

ROASTED FOX
How can we build a progressive cable TV network and connect liberal talk radio to our work in the field? Help write the business plan and strategic recipe to match what Roger Ailes has cooked up—using our best ingredients.

MEALS ON WHEELS
Remember that movie Bob Roberts and the mobile technology campaign vehicle? It's time to gas some up for our side—to drive effective "portable politics" in cities across America.

CLIFF'S VOTES
Busy people need "Cliffs Notes" scorecards and voter guides from trusted sources to help them wisely pick the right candidate. Groups like The League of Independent Voters, Rural Voters, and Hip Hop Voters will serve 'em up hot. In season.

MAIN DISHES
No fooling around. This is the meat.

MOVEON MISLEADER CAMPAIGN
Challenge the president every day, via the Internet, targeted TV & radio. Highly perishable if not eaten by Spring.

ACT/ AMERICA VOTES
A strategic effort to more effectively turn out voters in the key presidential states using canvassing, phone-banking and targeted mail. Ground by hand.

PRESIDENTIAL MEDIA FUND
In March, we'll probably have a nominee unable to afford TV to compete with Bush. This entrée supports production and placement of critical, swing-state television advertising.

CENTER FOR AMERICAN PROGRESS
A promising new think-tank for cooking up juicy, big ideas. Adapted from the "Heritage" recipe, first served in 1973.

GRASSROOTS DEMOCRATS
We can prevent another Florida. Look for a new network of poll watchers and political "taste testers." Available now.

NEW CANDIDATE RECRUITMENT
We've got new leaders, you just don't know them yet. Candidate recruitment, training and legislative support programs can fix this situation. Available from Progressive Majority, Wellstone Action and High Road Now.org.

REGIME CHANGE CAFÉ
HOT AND TASTY FARE FOR A HUNGRY PUBLIC

STAPLES
High in nutritional value. A must for any healthy progressive diet.

VITAMIN E-3
Chronic under-investment in education, smart economics and the environment is weakening America's bone structure. Get some spine at www.ourfuture.org. For an extra boost, try their New Growth Initiative.

REPUBLICAN ROLAIDS
While we countdown the days until November 2, stop George Bush and Tom Delay from passing more bad bills that undermine our health and welfare. Visit sites like TrueMajority.com, Seiu.org, and SaveBiogems.org to help stop the indigestion.

THE DAILY FEED
Ready for a provocative-not-preachy "progressive Paul Harvey" each day for 2 minutes? Fresh commentary from spunky creatives—hot off the griddle. Available for radio, Internet or TV. Content feedbags sold by the day or in bulk.

FOR DESSERT
BUSH FLAMBÉ
Sponsor efforts to dog President Bush's credibility at speaking events such as the proposed Liar Liar Pants on Fire campaign. In the spirit of Chicken George and Joe Tobacco.

BAKED APPLE
It's not too soon to adopt efforts to get under Republicans' skin at the NYC GOP Convention. Some special items you can order include:

- Buying a billboard on 34th Street
- Wrapping a sound truck or press bus
- Travel for the 2004 Convention Truth Squad

TAKE AND MAKE YOURSELF
Want to be your own block captain? Need a kit to hold a house party? Ready to start a local chapter for Progressive Majority or another worthy cause? A shrink-wrapped solution may be available.

READY TO ORDER?

visit www.regimechangecafe.com for weekly specials

Disclaimer: This unofficial menu is issued for entertainment purposes only. See your local Health Department or an attorney to ensure the sanctity of anything you wish to ingest.

CHAPTER 19
Organize, Don't Agonize

===========

"Where are the Democrats?" It has been a near universal complaint as the Right has been able to drive through remarkably destructive legislation despite razor-thin Republican majorities in the House and Senate. Rep. Jan Schakowsky is a leader of progressives in the House who has organized internally to get Democrats to stand up. Here, in an edited version of her remarks to the Take Back America Conference, she issues a challenge to the rest of us.

HOW BADLY DO YOU WANT IT?
by Representative Jan Schakowsky

DO YOU WANT A different president in 2004? Do you want to build a progressive majority? Do you want to change the direction of this country? I'm asking this as a serious question, not a rhetorical one. Do you want it badly enough to actually do what is necessary to win?

Everywhere I go, everywhere every Democrat goes, we hear, "Where are the Democrats?" I take that challenge seriously, and many of us are working day and night to make ourselves heard, putting together an inside/outside strategy with members who are willing to use tougher language and "creative" tactics in coordination with outside organizations.

We need more Democrats who believe, as Paul Wellstone

said, "the politics of conviction is a winning politics," but it takes more than the progressives now in office to make a change. Let me challenge you: "Where are you?" I say that as an activist and organizer myself and with a great deal of respect for the work that all of you are doing. I acknowledge the magnificent visibility of the antiwar activities, and the Web-based organizing that has generated millions of emails to Congress, the work of the Campaign for America's Future, the Anti-Tax Cut Coalition and others. I say that with enormous respect for the work of organized labor nationally and locally. I know we are all grateful to President John Sweeney of the AFL-CIO and his incredibly effective leadership.

Even so, too few viewpoints, other than those consistent with those of the administration, actually break through to the public. If we are to win, it's clear we need to do more, do it louder, do it faster, and do it better. And if we don't, in 2008 we will live in a country and a world far different from the one we have had and the one to which we aspire.

This president is seriously undermining the rule of law and the Constitution of the United States, precious civil liberties and doing it all in the name of patriotism. So where are the lawyers and judges? Why am I not hearing your protests, your emails and phone calls, your letters to the editor, your calls to talk radio, your high-profile lawsuits? This should be a bipartisan effort, one that stretches from left to right. Privacy is a major concern for average Americans and Big Brother is mining our most private information as we sit here. I realized how serious this was when a woman asked me how she could get another perspective on the Iraq war and I suggested a few Web sites. She asked me if she went there whether she would find herself on a list. In all honesty, I found that I couldn't say with confidence, "Absolutely not; this is still the United States of America and you can look at anything you want."

Lawyers, judges, where are you?

Seniors, where are you? I want to see sustained, loud, angry activity. The president just forced through a prescription drug bill that actually prohibits Medicare from negotiating on price with the drug companies. They turned a $400 billion program from a senior citizen benefit into a drug company subsidy, one that will lead to higher drug prices for all of us. The White House still works to privatize Social Security and Medicare and cut Medicaid. Conservatives force through tax cuts for the wealthy and help manufacture the fiscal crisis that forces cuts in those basic programs. It's a twofer for them.

Where are the veterans groups? For all the talk about patriotism, even veterans are taking a hit. Many veterans have to wait 15 months just to get an appointment with a doctor.

Environmentalists, Alaska is melting; the journal *Nature* reports that 90 percent of all large fish, such as tuna, marlin, swordfish, cod, and halibut, are gone from our oceans. The fuel efficiency of our cars is at a 22-year low. It's now considered patriotic, for crying out loud, to drive a Hummer. So where the hell are you? I want to read about you and join you protesting at hearings in Washington or Big Oil shareholder meetings. We need the activists and scientists to challenge this aggressively anti-science administration. Some things we may be able to reverse when we wrest power over the planet from their control. But extinct is extinct.

My sisters, where are the demonstrations against the war on women that is being waged every day in every way? This term, the Congress passed the ban on so-called partial birth abortion. Why is Congress outlawing a medical procedure about which it knows nothing? Because this is a thinly disguised assault on fundamental reproductive rights. On his first day in office, President Bush attacked the poorest most vulnerable women in the world when he cut U.S. family planning funds for organizations that have the gall to counsel, refer or, God forbid, perform abortions in countries where it is legal (which it happens to be in ours, by the way).

Our women in the military can't, with their own funds, have a safe and legal abortion at a military hospital, even if they are in Iraq or Saudi Arabia. A rabidly anti-choice man who thinks that women's health concerns can be cured with prayer is now on the Food and Drug Administration's Advisory Committee for Reproductive Health Drugs. They want to eliminate Title IX, equal opportunities for women in education and sports; they've done little to help victims of sexual assault and domestic violence. So sisters, where are you?

We all need to join in the efforts of organized labor on behalf of ALL working families in this country. In the dead of night, the Republican leadership and the president stripped from the year-end appropriations "omnibus" bill a measure that was passed by both Houses of Congress to overturn Labor Department rules that would strip about 8 million workers of the right to overtime. The first thing the White House did was throw out the workplace safety rules that would have protected workers from crippling repetitive motion injuries. Just picture another four years of a Bush administration unfettered by concerns of re-election. Unions are not in the 2008 picture. In 2008, there may not be any public employees let alone public employee unions. Everything will be privatized and contracted out. Private sector unions are already under siege. They face constant well-financed referenda in state after state, legal assaults and investigations at every level. So workers where are you?

I salute the leadership that the religious leaders—clergy and lay people—have shown in opposing the march to war in Iraq. Don't stop now. "God is a Republican" is a guiding principle for this administration. As long as there are Congressional resolutions and official days of prayer, the United States can continue to preemptively attack any country it wants. As Senate Leader Bill Frist said at a large gathering I attended, "All you need to know is the difference between right and wrong, good and evil."

Their God is homophobic and anti-choice. The Secretary of Education Rod Paige said, "All things equal, I would prefer to have a child in a school that has a strong appreciation for the values of the Christian community. In a religious environment the value system is set. That's not the case in a public school where there are so many different kids with different kinds of values." The dangerous destruction of the wall between Church and State is well under way. It is religious leaders and the faith community that need to address this.

Disability rights activists, immigrant advocates, housing advocates, civil rights leaders, gay and lesbian activists, all warriors for social and economic justice, thank you for what you do. And now we need to do more, do it louder, do it faster and do it better.

Clearly the Right has a number of tools at its disposal right now that we don't have.

1. They control the White House and are placing ideologues at every level of the administration, the Senate and House and much of the judiciary.

2. They control large swaths of the media and that creates a very effective echo chamber for all their initiatives and smear campaigns. And Federal Communications Commission wants to lift most restrictions on consolidation to allow the Foxification and Clear Channelization of even more.

3. They have most of the money, and their corporate agenda and tax cuts for the rich ensure that will continue.

4. They lie with impunity. Let's face it. They're liars. They lied about the reason they took our sons and daughters to war. They spend millions of dollars in campaign ads saying they are for a prescription drug benefit under Medicare while they work to destroy Medicare and replace it with private plans and HMOs. They call their dirty air legislation "Clear Skies" and their plan to give the timber companies our trees, "Healthy Forests." They call their job-killing economic program a "jobs program." They say they are for peace when they are for war. Millions of children are left behind under their miserly "No Child Left

Behind" education bill. They tout a child tax credit for working families and then silently drop it in favor of more tax cuts for millionaires.

5. And perhaps most important, they are unafraid and unabashed and unapologetic about pushing their right-wing agenda, no matter what. They are always playing offense. I used to think, oh they can't be serious about this or that—another huge tax cut, eliminating Title IX, continuing tax breaks for companies that move their offices to Bermuda, locking up immigrants indefinitely without due process, using Federal dollars to build churches—it's just a trial balloon. Forget that. They mean what they say and they don't give up until they get it. This is where we come in.

If we are serious about changing the course of this country, starting by getting rid of George W. Bush in 17 months, then we have to make some decisions and some commitments. During the war, a couple of nuns came to see me in my Chicago office. They were on their way to jail to serve a three-month sentence for an aggravated misdemeanor for protesting the School of the Americas in Fort Benning, Georgia. They crossed a line in the road and now they were going to prison. Think of it. Anyway, on their way to jail, they had been arrested on Lake Shore Drive in Chicago in an antiwar protest. The police got a bit carried away even though the 'City Council had passed a strong antiwar resolution.

The nuns wanted to know what could be done to change the state of affairs. I said I thought someone needed to take voter registration forms to every meeting and demonstration and get people fired up to vote. They said that would be hard. Why? Because people were fed up with the Democrats. I said, "Then they are going to have to Get Over It, and you are going to have to help them. Because like it or not, either George W. Bush or the Democratic nominee, whoever he or she may be, will be our next president."

All of you know who I'm talking about. I may be talking about you. We should, by all means, be working to promote a progressive agenda with each and every candidate and to make the nominee as progressive as possible.

But in the end, we are going to have to dedicate ourselves to winning elections. To do otherwise is a luxury we cannot afford. I look forward to our campaign for a universal health care plan or a real education bill or labor law reform. We cannot even have that conversation now. We are trying to hang on by our fingernails to what we have now. And we are losing.

The good news today is that we have them on the run on several fronts. The president is touting the recovery, but it hasn't reached working families yet. Most of them are getting hit with tax hikes and service cuts at the local level that cost a lot more than the token tax breaks they got from the president's plan.

The missing weapons of mass destruction are becoming a real annoyance to them now, and the media is starting to pick it up. More and more members of Congress, even some Republicans, are asking for investigations. Editorial boards are beginning to write about it. The arrogance that placed our troops at risk in Iraq without adequate training or equipment in an occupation that was supposed to be a celebration is raising severe doubts about this White House's foreign policy.

We need to take advantage of these opportunities. The polls tell us that the president is in fact vulnerable. His re-elect numbers are not that great. We have to do with fervor what we already know how to do. We have to register base voters who have left us at least in part because they think we don't speak to them. And here you have another choice. You can bitch that the Democrats don't speak to them, or you can speak to them, one on one, door-to-door, worker-to-worker, meeting after meeting, neighbor to neighbor. Set a goal for yourself, personally, perhaps, 100 new progressive voters between now and Election Day.

Become part of a progressive echo chamber. When the Republicans go after Tom Daschle or Nancy Pelosi for being unpatriotic when they criticize the president, Fox News and Rush Limbaugh begin spinning the same line. We need to push back, writing letters to the editor, calling talk shows, emailing Congress, challenging the Right and telling them they are out of line, calling *them* un-American for stifling dissent.

When conservatives launch a really bad proposal or progressives a good one, we need to have coordinated efforts throughout the country. We need to use our think tanks and grassroots and Web-based organizations in increasingly creative ways and coordinate that with activities of the progressive Democrats who are becoming more and more vocal in the Congress.

We have one great advantage. We can tell the truth. We don't need to lie or hide. Our polices are better for Americans—for their health and well-being, for their kids' education and their family budget, and White House re-election propaganda notwithstanding, for our nation's security, our country's prosperity and our hopes for raising our children in peaceful world.

So continue to challenge us to do better. Hold us accountable; push us hard. But don't stop there. Look in that mirror. Hold yourself accountable. Push yourself to do more than you have ever done. If we are to rid ourselves of this burden, we will have to lift together.

CHAPTER 20
Put the Whole Team on the Field

Trained at the side of Dr. Martin Luther King, Rev. Jesse L. Jackson has long been a leader of the social justice movements. His presidential campaigns in 1984 and 1988 demonstrated the potential of a coalition across lines of race based upon economic common ground. Now, in updated and revised excerpts from remarks at the Take Back America Conference, he calls on progressives to unite. Against conventional wisdom, he urges progressives to take the offensive in the "red zone," the states of the South and Southwest, arguing that forty years after the Voting Rights Act, it is time to build a majority coalition for change.

BRING THE FAMILY TOGETHER
by the Reverend Jesse L. Jackson

AS WE HEAD INTO this election, there is much talk about what a winning message is. I don't think it is all that complicated. We know what it is. The message should come out of what's right for our people. The good news is the message can work for us. The message is not tax-and-spend Democrats. It's not slash-and-burn Republicans. Our message is invest and grow in shared economic security.

Invest and grow in shared economic security. Invest in public schools. Invest in public housing, affordable housing.

Invest in college tuition. Invest in public infrastructure. Invest in 12 million children. Invest in teacher training. Invest in Head Start. Invest in high-tech skills. Let's invest and grow. Invest and grow and put America back to work. We don't need to give back to those already in the surplus. We need to invest in the potential of those in need. Invest to close the vertical gap, to close the digital divide, to close the North/South gap, to close the gap between the surplus culture and the deficit culture.

There is an inverse correlation between investing in Head Start and prenatal care on the frontside and poverty and welfare on the backside. Investing on the frontside is morally right—and it costs less, too. We can ensure that every child gets a healthy start and comes to school ready to learn, or we can pay a lot more on the backside dealing with those who never had a chance. This isn't rocket science; it is just common sense.

We can get beyond the race divide. We can take away race-baiting wages. We can take away the fears that divide people huddling in hunger and deprivation. Most poor people are not black. They are white, single, female, and young. More whites live in poverty than there are blacks in America. A coal miner dies every six hours from black lung disease. Most poor folks are not on welfare. They work every day. Speak to them. They'll vote for us.

The challenge isn't really about message. The challenge is about mobilization and moving together. The hard task for our coalition is to heal, to build and to come together. When I ran for president in 1988, I would always tell the story of my grandmother. We were poor, so she used to sew together patches of many colors and shapes to make a quilt to keep us warm in the winter. Even in South Carolina, it got cold in the winter. So my grandmother took the rejected scraps— the old rags, the discarded refuse—and used strong thread to tie them together into a thing of beauty and warmth. Many colors, many textures bound together to a mighty quilt. And that's a lesson for us: the rejected stones of America can become the cornerstones of a new America.

There's another lesson for us from my grandmother's quilt. All of the patches had their place. If any patch were missing, the cold air would come through the weak part and freeze us at night. But none of the patches was big enough to cover us by itself. All the patches needed all the other patches to work to keep us warm. Liberals, you are right in your analysis, but your patch is not big enough. Union members, you are right, but your patch is not big enough. African Americans, your claim is right, but you are not strong enough alone. Latinos, you are right, and your patch is getting bigger every day, but it is still not big enough. Women, you are rising, but your patch is not big enough. Peace activists, you are brave and you fought hard. We turned out 15 million on February 15, all over the world, but our patch is still not strong enough. Gays and lesbians, you are strong, but your patch is not big enough. We must come together. Many patches, strong thread, a thing of beauty, a thing of strength. . . .

To do this, we must rise above our prior divisions and put aside past bitterness. We must open the Democratic door wide open to Ralph Nader and the Greens. We need those three million votes. We cannot leave any element of our family behind and win. We need the black trade unionists.

NAACP. Appalachian coal families. Native Americans. DNC. The family must function under one big tent. The big challenge is to heal and to build.

And often that requires swallowing our pride to move forward. In 1992, Bill Clinton's staff set me up for a deliberate snub at my convention—the infamous Sister Souljah incident. In the aftermath of that insult, I had three basic choices. I could, in my bruised feelings, pout and sit out the 1992 election, and give just a little more support to George senior, de facto. I could exact payback, entering the race as a fourth party candidate. Remember at that point, Perot was leading and Clinton was running third. Or I could take the long view about what was good for our party and good for our people, accept Clinton's prompt apology, and move on.

The first two would have provided personal gratification but would have hurt our team. The stakes were too high to allow private pain to outweigh the need for public policy. And so I took the hit, and then I did more that fall to register and mobilize voters than anyone but the candidate himself. That was the right decision for 1992.

Now I ask you to make a similar and difficult decision. Those of you who voted for Al Gore in 2000, as I did, must let go of your anger, and must reach out to rebuild one big tent. Those of you who supported Nader in 2000, release your pain. Don't embrace your isolation, seek instead the possibility that can come from coming together. Iran and Iraq are just two of the many good reasons to come back home. For the sake of whatever little children will get bombed next by the chickenhawks, let's come together. Let us have all our forces in the field to defend ourselves against these ruthless would-be emperors. We are going to need every patch if we are to fend off the cold.

The stakes are very high. These are not your father's conservatives. The ideologues around George Bush aren't his father's conservatives. They have shown repeatedly how radical their program is and how ruthless their politics are. They expropriated an election in Florida in 2000. They manipulated an election in 2002. If they fall behind in 2004, don't be surprised if they engineer another big threat to try to scare everyone into line by election day. They've lied about the threat from Iraq. They manufactured evidence and exaggerated rumor to make their case. Now they are saying that it doesn't matter whether they told the truth or not. They believe their mission is so worthy, and their right to rule so inherited, that they can lie, slander, or mislead if necessary to get their way. This is the attitude of czars, not of presidents.

So we must come together. But if we are to stand together, we must stand for something. Unity is not forged around a least common denominator. Unity is forged by a higher vision and a common ground. Don't be too quick to abandon your principles in the search for a winner. Sometimes, as Paul Wellstone taught us, the principles are what makes the winner. As Jim Hightower said, every now and then a politician should do something just because it's right and that's enough. We want to make America better, not simply change the names in the White House or the Congress.

And to do that, we need to mobilize for 2004, but build for the long term, for much more than one election. We need to reach out and speak to the needs and the hopes of our people. That way, whether we win in 2004 or not, we can continue to build and continue to make a difference. In 1988, many people said that I was the best candidate, had the best ideas, had won all or most of the debates, had the most votes from a rainbow of voters, and even managed to raise millions of dollars which no one believed we could do. But, they said, Jackson can't win. I did not get the nomination, but our campaign opened up new possibilities. In 1984, our campaign helped register two million new voters. In 1986, we took back the Senate while Ronald Reagan was at the height of his popularity. Winning has many manifestations. In 1988, I won thirteen primaries and caucuses and seven million votes and more delegates than any runner-up ever, but they said I still couldn't win. But the votes and forces we helped unleash within our party helped elect the first African-American governor of Virginia, the first African-American mayor of New York, the most rainbow U.S. Congress in history, the first African-American female senator, and helped Bill Clinton and Al Gore win the popular vote three straight times. Neither Clinton nor Gore won the majority white vote, even with the gender gap. The margin of victory came from African Americans and Latinos, as it will in the year 2004.

Corporate Democrats like to argue that we have to dampen our hopes and curb our tongues to appeal to the "center," the "swing voter." But the swing voters have many of the same hopes that we have. And we can lose more swing votes from those who stay home in despair than from those who allow old divisions to scare them away. We must make certain when we build our quilt that we include patches of every color and every texture. We have to reach out systematically, not simply symbolically, invest resources, attention, advertising, programs. We want to take back America, but never forget that some of the people who we need, people who built America, never had the chance to own that much of America to take back in the first place.

Here we can learn much from Paul Wellstone. Paul not only talked the talk, he walked the walk. In 1987, he defied popular wisdom and party bureaucrats to manage my campaign in Minnesota. That helped him put together the team and the organizers that allowed him to defeat an incumbent for the U.S. Senate seat, a seat he would have kept today were he not taken from us. To build a big quilt in 1987, Paul Wellstone crossed the color line and endorsed me for president. The smart plan would have been Simon or Dukakis. But Paul took a risk—a risk for principle—and, three years later, he won a seat in the U.S. Senate. He was the only Democrat to defeat an incumbent GOP senator in that year. A lesson for our times.

Paul's lesson of crossing the color line is especially important now. Because the road to an enduring progressive majority lies through the so-called "red states," the supposed Republican bastions in the South and Southwest. The once Democratic solid South has become the totally Republican solid South. But we can win in those states. To do so, we must cross the color line. To win in the South, we must register the hundreds of thousands of African Americans and thousands of new Latino residents. And then we must bridge the gulf between whites and black, and move beyond racial battlegrounds to economic common ground. . . .

Bridge that gulf, and we can win. In 2000, Al Gore got cheated out of Florida by Katherine Harris, a butterfly ballot, uncounted votes on some old and tired voting machines, a partisan decision by five Supreme Court injustices, and a concerted effort to disenfranchise African-American voters. We lost the governor's race in South Carolina by 40,000 votes; 400,000 blacks unregistered. We lost the Senate vote in Georgia by 50,000 votes; 600,000 blacks unregistered.

What do blacks and whites in the South have in common beyond pulling for the same team at the football game? In the football stands, there are black and white mothers and fathers on both sides. They have moved beyond skin color to uniform color. What do they have in common besides the football field? The need for health care and pensions. The need for retirement security. The need for high-quality public education for all children. George Bush is offering the photo ops, an empire, tax cuts, and the fear of terrorism. Our agenda is better for them, for their families, and the future of their children.

So we should systematically begin working in the red zone. In football, twenty yards and in from a touchdown is called the red zone. That's where picking up yards gets tough. Many teams are very good around the fifty-yard line, when defenses are spread out, but have little stomach for the red zone where everything is tougher.

In some ways, the South has ever been our red zone. In the 1960s, the struggle for public accommodations, the right to vote, to break down the cotton curtain, came from the South. The civil rights movement had to overcome deep-seated fears, violent resistance, and entrenched opposition in the red zone. Then, as apartheid was finally eliminated in law, much of the white majority responded in fear. Republicans played on those fears, offering themselves as the party of white sanctuary and benefiting from a massive shift of whites toward the Southern Republican party.

When Lyndon Johnson signed the Voting Rights Act, he said we've lost the South for a generation. That was forty years ago. Now it is time to go back into the red zone and challenge that racial divide. Many Southerners can't afford to vote Republican. They are not wealthy. Their jobs are in jeopardy. Their kids go to substandard schools. Their jobs do not pay health insurance or a living wage. They have nothing to gain from all those tax shelters and tax rebates to the top 1 percent. Half of all the toxic waste dumps are in the South, in their neighborhoods. The most uninsured seniors, the most uninsured women live there, the biggest education gaps are there, yet they are driven by fear to vote against their own interests in the red zone. We must reach out to them, and lead them from racial battlegrounds to economic common ground.

If we are going to succeed—not just in one election but to make this country better—we have to march through the red zone. And the closer we get, the more intense is the resistance we'll face. You saw that in Texas, where Republican Majority leader Tom DeLay trampled the voting rights of Latinos and African Americans to gerrymander new districts for Republicans. Sometimes we will have to attack, and sometimes defend. We must never allow Tom DeLay and Karl Rove to use our dreams as punching bags or treat our allies like sitting ducks. Politics is a contact sport. When one of us is attacked, we must all strike back. Never again should we allow the right wing to compare Tom Daschle to Saddam Hussein, while we just sit quietly. We have to stand up and fight back.

Finally, it's time to march again. We've lost three million jobs in two years. We've lost $5 trillion in stock value. Billions in 401(K) plans decimated. Pension plans stolen. Enron, Halliburton, MCI, World/Com. Scandals, immorality. No enforcement of OSHA or EPA. We must march again. We've lost jobs: in Massachusetts, in California. In North Carolina. In Ohio and Michigan. It's time for a workers' march.

It's time to march across these states in a gigantic march on Washington. A working-people's march on Washington. The sophisticates say marching doesn't matter, but they're wrong. Marching does matter. Marching inspires us. . . . The more you march, the better you feel. . . . It wakes up sleeping people. . . . It worked for Moses. . . . It worked for Joshua. . . . It worked for Gandhi. . . . It worked for Martin Luther King. . . . .In the spring of 1968, Dr. King was killed. On June 5, 1968, Robert Kennedy was killed. Last year, Paul and Sheila Wellstone were killed. And so, Dr. King cannot march today. Paul and Sheila cannot march today. Robert Kennedy cannot march today. We who are in that tradition, march for them. March for the future. March for hope. Keep hope alive. March on.

SECTION VIII

THE STAKES

CHAPTER 21
The Progressive Story of America

═══════════

In June, the Campaign for America's Future awarded Bill Moyers its Lifetime Achievement Award, honoring a lifetime of independent, honest, path-breaking journalism. At the awards dinner, Moyers delivered a remarkable oration, placing today's struggles in their historic context, providing enlightenment and inspiration to all.

ACCEPTANCE OF AMERICA'S FUTURE LIFETIME LEADERSHIP AWARD
by Bill Moyers

THANK YOU FOR THIS award and for this occasion. I don't deserve either, but as George Burns said, I have arthritis and I don't deserve that, either.

Tomorrow is my sixty-ninth birthday and I cannot imagine a better present than this award or a better party than your company.

Fifty-three years ago tomorrow, on my sixteenth birthday, I went to work for the daily newspaper in the small east Texas town where I grew up. It was a good place to be a cub reporter—small enough to navigate but big enough to keep me busy and learning something every day. I soon had a stroke of luck. Some of the old-timers were on vacation or out sick and I got assigned to cover what came to be known as the Housewives' Rebellion. Fifteen women in my hometown decided not to pay the Social Security withholding tax for their domestic workers. They argued that Social Security was unconstitutional, that imposing it was taxation without representation, and that—here's my favorite part— "requiring us to collect (the tax) is no different from requiring us to collect the garbage." They hired themselves a lawyer—none other than Martin Dies, the former congressman best known, or worst known, for his work as head of the House Committee on Un-American Activities in the '30s and '40s. He was no more effective at defending rebellious women than he had been protecting against communist subversives, and eventually the women wound up holding their noses and paying the tax.

The stories I wrote for my local paper were picked up and moved on the Associated Press wire. One day the managing editor called me over and pointed to the AP ticker beside his desk. Moving across the wire was a notice citing one Bill Moyers and the paper for the reporting we had done on the "Rebellion." That hooked me, and in one way or another— after a detour through seminary and then into politics and government for a spell—I've been covering the class war ever since. Those women in Marshall, Texas, were its advance guard. They were not bad people. They were regulars at church, their children were my friends, many of them were active in community affairs, their husbands were pillars of the business and professional class in town. They were respectable and upstanding citizens all. So it took me a while to figure out what had brought on that spasm of reactionary rebellion. It came to me one day, much later. They simply couldn't see beyond their own prerogatives. Fiercely loyal to their families, to their clubs, charities, and congregations—fiercely loyal, in other words, to their own kind—they narrowly defined membership in democracy to include only people like them. The women who washed and ironed their laundry, wiped their children's bottoms, made their husband's beds, and cooked their family meals—these women, too, would grow old and frail, sick and decrepit, lose their husbands and face the ravages of time alone, with nothing to show from their years of labor but the crease in their brow and the knots on their knuckles; so be it; even on the distaff side of laissez-faire, security was personal, not social, and what injustice existed this side of heaven would no doubt be redeemed beyond the Pearly Gates. God would surely be just to the poor once they got past Judgment Day. In one way or another, this is the oldest story in America: the struggle to determine whether "we, the people" is a spiritual idea embedded in a political reality— one nation, indivisible—or merely a charade masquerading as piety and manipulated by the powerful and privileged to sustain their own way of life at the expense of others.

Let me make it clear that I don't harbor any idealized notion of politics and democracy; I worked for Lyndon Johnson, remember? Nor do I romanticize "the people." You should read my mail—or listen to the vitriol virtually spat at my answering machine. I understand what the politician meant who said of the Texas House of Representatives, "If you think these guys are bad, you should see their constituents." But there is nothing idealized or romantic about the difference between a society whose arrangements roughly serve all its citizens and one whose institutions have been converted into a stupendous fraud. That difference can be the difference between democracy and oligarchy.

Look at our history. All of us know that the American Revolution ushered in what one historian called "The Age of Democratic Revolutions." For the Great Seal of the United States the new Congress went all the way back to the Roman poet Virgil: *Novus Ordo Seclorum*—"a new age now begins." Page Smith reminds us that "their ambition was not merely to free themselves from dependence and subordination to the Crown but to inspire people everywhere to create agencies of government and forms of common social life that would offer greater dignity and hope to the exploited and suppressed"— to those, in other words, who had been the losers. Not surprisingly, the winners often resisted. In the early years of constitution-making in the states and emerging nation, aristocrats wanted a government of propertied "gentlemen" to keep the scales tilted in their favor. Battling on the other side were moderates and even those radicals harboring the extraordinary idea of letting all white males have the vote. Luckily, the weapons were words and ideas, not bullets. Through compromise and conciliation the draftsmen achieved a Constitution of checks and balances that is now the oldest in the world, even as the revolution of democracy that inspired it remains a tempestuous adolescent whose destiny is still up for grabs. For all the rhetoric about "life, liberty, and the pursuit of happiness," it took a civil war to free the slaves and another hundred years to invest their freedom with meaning. Women only gained the right to vote in my mother's time. New ages don't arrive overnight, or without "blood, sweat, and tears."

You know this. You are the heirs of one of the country's great traditions—the Progressive movement that started late in the nineteenth century and remade the American experience piece by piece until it peaked in the last third of the twentieth century. I call it the Progressive movement for lack of a more precise term. Its aim was to keep blood pumping through the veins of democracy when others were ready to call in the mortician. Progressives exalted and extended the original American Revolution. They spelled out new terms of partnership between the people and their rulers. And they kindled a flame that lit some of the most prosperous decades in modern history, not only here but in aspiring democracies everywhere, especially those of Western Europe.

Step back with me to the curtain-raiser, the founding convention of the People's Party—better known as the Populists—in 1892. The members were mainly cotton and wheat farmers from the recently reconstructed South and the newly settled Great Plains, and they had come on hard, hard times, driven to the wall by falling prices for their crops on one hand and racking interest rates, freight charges, and supply costs on the other. This in the midst of a booming and growing industrial America. They were angry, and their platform—issued deliberately on the Fourth of July—pulled no punches. "We meet," it said, "in the midst of a nation brought to the verge of moral, political and material ruin. . . . Corruption dominates the ballot box, the [state] legislatures and the Congress and touches even the bench. . . . The newspapers are largely subsidized or muzzled, public opinion silenced. . . . The fruits of the toil of millions are boldly stolen to build up colossal fortunes for a few."

Furious words from rural men and women who were traditionally conservative and invoked an American tradition as powerful as frontier individualism—the war on inequality and especially on the role that government played in promoting and preserving inequality by favoring the rich. The Founding Fathers turned their backs on the idea of property qualifications for holding office under the Constitution because they wanted no part of a "veneration for wealth" in the document. Thomas Jefferson, while claiming no interest in politics, built up a Republican party—no relation to the present one—to take the government back from the speculators and "stock-jobbers," as he called them, who were in the saddle in 1800. Andrew Jackson slew the monster Second Bank of the United States, the 600-pound gorilla of the credit system in the 1830s, in the name of the people versus the aristocrats who sat on the bank's governing board.

All these leaders were on record in favor of small government—but their opposition wasn't simply to government as such. It was to government's power to confer privilege on insiders; on the rich who were democracy's equivalent of the royal favorites of monarchist days. (It's what the FCC does today.) The Populists knew it was the government that granted millions of acres of public land to the railroad builders. It was the government that gave the manufacturers of farm machinery a monopoly of the domestic market by a protective tariff that was no longer necessary to shelter "infant industries." It was the government that contracted the national currency and sparked a deflationary cycle that crushed debtors and fattened the wallets of creditors. And those who made the great fortunes used them to buy the legislative and judicial favors that kept them on top. So the Populists recognized one great principle: the job of preserving equality of opportunity and democracy demanded the end of any unholy alliance between government and wealth. It was, to quote that platform again, "from the same womb of *governmental injustice*" that tramps and millionaires were bred. But how? How was the democratic revolution to be revived? The promise of the Declaration reclaimed? How were Americans to restore government to its job of promoting the *general* welfare? And here, the Populists made a breakthrough to another principle. In a modern, large-scale, industrial and nationalized economy it wasn't enough simply to curb the government's outreach. That would simply leave power in the hands of the great corporations whose existence was inseparable from growth and progress. The answer was to turn government into an active player in the economy at the very least enforcing fair play, and—when necessary—being the friend, the helper, and the agent of the people at large in the contest against entrenched power. So the Populist platform called for government loans to farmers about to lose their mortgaged homesteads—for government granaries to grade and store their crops fairly—for governmental inflation of the currency, which was a classical plea of debtors, and for some decidedly nonclassical actions like government ownership of the railroad, telephone, and telegraph systems, and a graduated—that is, progressive—tax on incomes and a flat ban on subsidies to "any private corporation." And to make sure the government stayed on the side of the people, the "Pops" called for the initiative and referendum and the direct election of Senators. Predictably, the Populists were denounced, feared, and mocked as fanatical hayseeds ignorantly playing with socialist fire. They got twenty-two electoral votes for their candidate in '92, plus some Congressional seats and state houses, but it was downhill from there for many reasons. America wasn't—and probably still isn't—ready for a new major party. The People's Party was a spent rocket by 1904. But if political organizations perish, their key ideas don't—keep that in mind, because it gives prospective to your cause today. Much of the Populist agenda would become law within a few years of the party's extinction. And that was because it was generally shared by a rising generation of young Republicans and Democrats who, justly or not, were seen as less outrageously outdated than the embattled farmers. These were the progressives, your intellectual forebears and mine.

One of my heroes in all of this is William Allen White, a Kansas country editor—a Republican—who was one of them. He described his fellow progressives this way: "What the people felt about the vast injustice that had come with the settlement of a continent, we, their servants— teachers, city councilors, legislators, governors, publishers, editors, writers, representatives in Congress and Senators— all made a part of our creed. Some way, into the hearts of the dominant middle class of this country, had come a sense that their civilization needed recasting, that their government had fallen into the hands of self-seekers, that a new relationship should be established between the haves and the have-nots." They were a diverse lot, held together by a common admiration of progress—hence the name—and a shared dismay at the paradox of poverty stubbornly persisting in the midst of progress like an unwanted guest at a wedding. Of course they welcomed, just as we do, the new marvels in the gift-bag of technology—the telephones, the autos, the electrically-powered urban transport and lighting systems, the indoor heating and plumbing, the processed foods and home appliances and machine-made clothing that reduced the sweat and drudgery of home-making and were affordable to an ever-swelling number of people. But they saw the underside, too—the slums lurking in the shadows of the glittering cities, the exploited and unprotected workers whose low-paid labor filled the horn of plenty for others, the misery of those whom age, sickness, accident or hard times condemned to servitude and poverty with no hope of comfort or security.

This is what's hard to believe—hardly a century had passed since 1776 before the still young revolution was being strangled in the hard grip of a merciless ruling class. The large corporations that were called into being by modern industrialism after 1865—the end of the Civil War—had combined into trusts capable of making minions of both politics and government. What Henry George called "an immense wedge" was being forced through American society by "the maldistribution of wealth, status, and opportunity."

We should pause here to consider that this is Karl Rove's cherished period of American history; it was, as I read him, the seminal influence on the man who is said to be George W.'s brain. From his own public comments and my reading of the record, it is apparent that Karl Rove has modeled the Bush presidency on that of William McKinley, who was in the White House from 1897 to 1901, and modeled himself on Mark Hanna, the man who virtually manufactured McKinley. Hanna had one consummate passion—to serve corporate and imperial power. It was said that he believed "without compunction, that the state of Ohio existed for property. It had no other function. . . . Great wealth was to be gained through monopoly, through using the State for private ends; it was axiomatic therefore that businessmen should run the government and run it for personal profit." Mark Hanna—Karl Rove's hero—made William McKinley governor of Ohio by shaking down the corporate interests of the day. Fortunately, McKinley had the invaluable gift of emitting sonorous platitudes as though they were recently discovered truth. Behind his benign gaze the wily intrigues of Mark Hanna saw to it that first Ohio and then Washington were "ruled by business . . . by bankers, railroads, and public utility corporations." Any who opposed the oligarchy were smeared as disturbers of the peace, socialists, anarchists, "or worse." Back then they didn't bother with hollow euphemisms like "compassionate conservatism" to disguise the raw reactionary politics that produced government "of, by, and for" the ruling corporate class. They just saw the loot and went for it.

The historian Clinton Rossiter describes this as the period of "the great train robbery of American intellectual history." Conservatives—or better, pro-corporate apologists—hijacked the vocabulary of Jeffersonian liberalism and tuurned words like "progress," "opportunity," and "individualism" into tools for making the plunder of America sound like divine right. Charles Darwin's theory of evolution was hijacked, too, so that conservative politicians, judges, and publicists promoted, as if it were, the natural order of things, the notion that progress resulted from the elimination of the weak and the "survival of the fittest." This "degenerate and unlovely age," as one historian calls it, exists in the mind of Karl Rove—the reputed brain of George W. Bush—as the seminal age of inspiration for the politics and governance of America today. No wonder that what troubled our progressive forebears was not only the miasma of poverty in their nostrils, but the sour stink of a political system for sale. The United States Senate was a "millionaire's club." Money given to the political machines that controlled nominations could buy controlling influence in city halls, state houses, and even courtrooms. Reforms and improvements ran into the immovable resistance of the almighty dollar. What, progressives wondered, would this do to the principles of popular government? Because all of them, whatever party they subscribed to, were inspired by the gospel of democracy. Inevitably, this swept them into the currents of politics, whether as active officeholders or persistent advocates. Here's a small, but representative sampling of their ranks. Jane Addams forsook the comforts of a middle-class college graduate's life to live in Hull House in the midst of a disease-ridden and crowded Chicago immigrant neighborhood, determined to make it an educational and social center that would bring pride, health, and beauty into the lives of her poor neighbors. She was inspired by "an almost passionate devotion to the ideals of democracy," to combating the prevailing notion "that the well-being of a privileged few might justly be built upon the ignorance and sacrifice of the many." Community and fellowship were the lessons she drew from her teachers, Jesus and Abraham Lincoln. But people simply helping one another couldn't move mountains of disadvantage. She came to see that "private beneficence" wasn't enough. But to bring justice to the poor would take more than soup kitchens and fund-raising prayer meetings. "Social arrangements," she wrote, "can be transformed through man's conscious and deliberate effort." Take note—not individual regeneration or the magic of the market, but conscious, cooperative effort. Meet a couple of muckraking journalists. Jacob Riis lugged his heavy camera up and down the staircases of New York's disease-ridden, firetrap tenements to photograph the unspeakable crowding, the inadequate toilets, the starved and hollow-eyed children and the filth on the walls so thick that his crude flash equipment sometimes set it afire. Bound between hard covers, with Riis's commentary, they showed comfortable New Yorkers *How the Other Half Lives*. They were powerful ammunition for reformers who eventually brought an end to tenement housing by state legislation. And Lincoln Steffens, college- and graduate-school educated, left his books to learn life from the bottom up as a police-beat reporter on New York's streets. Then, as a magazine writer, he exposed the links between city bosses and businessmen that made it possible for builders and factory owners to ignore safety codes and get away with it. But the villain was neither the boodler nor the businessman. It was the indifference of a public that "deplore[d] our politics and laud[ed] our business"; that transformed law, medicine, literature, and religion into simply business. Steffens was out to slay the dragon of exalting "the commercial spirit" over the goals of patriotism and national prosperity. "I am not a scientist," he said. "I am a journalist. I did not gather the facts and arrange them patiently for permanent preservation and laboratory analysis . . . . My purpose was . . . to see if the shameful facts, spread out in all their shame, would not burn through our civic shamelessness and set fire to American pride." If corrupt politics bred diseases that could be fatal to democracy, then good politics was the antidote. That was the discovery of Ray Stannard Baker, another journalistic progressive who started out with a detest for election-time catchwords and slogans. But he came to see that, "Politics could not be abolished or even adjourned . . . it was in its essence the method by which communities worked out their common problems. It was one of the principle arts of living peacefully in a crowded world," he said. (Compare that to Grover Norquist's latest declaration of war on the body politic. "We are trying to change the tones in the state capitals— and turn them toward bitter nastiness and partisanship." He went on to say that "bipartisanship is another name for date rape.") There are more, too many more to call to the witness stand here, but I want you to hear some of the things they had to say. There were educators like the economist John R. Commons or the sociologist Edward A. Ross who believed that the function of "social science" wasn't simply to dissect society for nonjudgmental analysis and academic promotion, but to help in finding solutions to social problems. It was Ross who pointed out that morality in a modern world had a social dimension. In *Sin and Society,* written in 1907, he told readers that the sins "blackening the face of our time" were of a new variety, and not yet recognized as such. "The man who picks pockets with a railway rebate, murders with an adulterant instead of a bludgeon, burglarizes with a 'rake-off' instead of a jimmy, cheats with a company instead of a deck of cards, or scuttles his town instead of his ship, does not feel on his brow the brand of a malefactor." In other words, upstanding individuals could plot corporate crimes and sleep the sleep of the just without the sting of social stigma or the pangs of conscience. Like Kenneth Lay, they could even be invited into the White House to write their own regulations. And here are just two final bits of testimony from actual politicians—first, Brand Whitlock, mayor of Toledo. He is one of my heroes because he first learned his politics as a beat reporter in Chicago, confirming my own experience that there's nothing better than journalism to turn life into a continuing course in adult education. One of his lessons was that "the alliance between the lobbyists and the lawyers of the great corporation interests on the one hand, and the managers of both the great political parties on the other, was a fact, the worst feature of which was that no one seemed to care."

And then there is Tom Johnson, the progressive mayor of Cleveland in the early 1900s—a businessman converted to social activism. His major battles were to impose regulation, or even municipal takeover, on the private companies that were meant to provide affordable public transportation and utilities but in fact crushed competitors, overcharged customers, secured franchises and licenses for a song, and paid virtually nothing in taxes—all through their pocketbook control of lawmakers and judges. Johnson's argument for public ownership was simple: "If you don't own them, they will own you. It's why advocates of Clean Elections today argue that

if anybody's going to buy Congress, it should be the people."
When advised that businessmen got their way in Washington because they had lobbies and consumers had none,
Tom Johnson responded: "If Congress were true to the principles of democracy it would be the people's lobby." What a
radical contrast to the House of Representatives today! Our
political, moral, and intellectual forbearance occupy a long
and honorable roster. They include wonderful characters
like Dr. Alice Hamilton, a pioneer in industrially caused diseases, who spent long years clambering up and down ladders
in factories and mineshafts—in long skirts!—tracking down
the unsafe toxic substances that sickened the workers whom
she would track right into their sickbeds to get leads and tip-
offs on where to hunt. Or Harvey Wiley, the chemist from
Indiana who, from a bureaucrat's desk in the Department of
Agriculture, relentlessly warred on foods laden with risky
preservatives and adulterants with the help of his "poison
squad" of young assistants who volunteered as guinea pigs.
Or lawyers like the brilliant Harvard graduate Louis Brandeis, who took on corporate attorneys defending child labor
or long and harsh conditions for female workers. Brandeis
argued that the state had a duty to protect the health of
working women and children.

To be sure, these progressives weren't all saints. Their
glory years coincided with the heyday of lynching and segregation, of empire and the Big Stick and the bold theft of the
Panama Canal, of immigration restriction and ethnic stereo-
types. Some were themselves businessmen only hoping to
control an unruly marketplace by regulation. But by and
large they were conservative reformers. They aimed to preserve

the existing balance between wealth and commonwealth. Their common enemy was unchecked privilege, their common hope was a better democracy, and their common weapon was informed public opinion. In a few short years the progressive spirit made possible the election not only of reform mayors and governors but of national figures like Senator George Norris of Nebraska, Senator Robert M. LaFollette of Wisconsin, and even that hard-to-classify political genius, Theodore Roosevelt. All three of them Republicans. Here is the simplest laundry-list of what was accomplished at state and federal levels: Publicly regulated or owned transportation, sanitation and utilities systems. The partial restoration of competition in the marketplace through improved antitrust laws. Increased fairness in taxation. Expansion of the public education and juvenile justice systems. Safer workplaces and guarantees of compensation to workers injured on the job. Oversight of the purity of water, medicines, and foods. Conservation of the national wilderness heritage against overdevelopment, and honest bidding on any public mining, lumbering, and ranching. We take these for granted today—or we did until recently. All were provided not by the automatic workings of free enterprise but by implementing the idea in the Declaration of Independence that the people had a right to governments that best promoted their "safety and happiness."

The mighty progressive wave peaked in 1912. But the ideas leashed by it forged the politics of the twentieth century. Like his cousin Theodore, Franklin Roosevelt argued that the real enemy of enlightened capitalism was "the malefactors of great wealth"—the "economic royalists"—from whom capitalism would have to be saved by reform and regulation. Progressive government became an embedded tradition of Democrats—the heart of FDR's New Deal and Harry Truman's Fair Deal, and honored even by Dwight D. Eisenhower, who didn't want to tear down the house progressive ideas had built—only to put it under different managers. The progressive impulse had its final fling in the landslide of 1969 when LBJ, who was a son of the west Texas hill country, where the Populist rebellion had been nurtured in the 1890s, won the public endorsement for what he meant to be the capstone in the arch of the New Deal. I had a modest role in that era. I shared in its exhilaration and its failures. We went too far too fast, overreached at home and in Vietnam, failed to examine some assumptions, and misjudged the rising discontents and fierce backlash engendered by war, race, civil disturbance, violence, and crime. Democrats grew so proprietary in this town that a fat, complacent political establishment couldn't recognize its own intellectual bankruptcy or the beltway that was growing around it and beginning to separate it from the rest of the country. The failure of Democratic politicians and public thinkers to respond to popular discontents—to the daily lives of workers, consumers, parents, and ordinary taxpayers—allowed a resurgent conservatism to convert public concern and hostility into a crusade to resurrect social Darwinism as a moral philosophy, multinational corporations as a governing class, and the theology of markets as a transcendental belief system.

As a citizen I don't like the consequences of this crusade, but you have to respect the conservatives for their successful strategy in gaining control of the national agenda. Their

stated and open aim is to change how America is governed—
to strip from government all its functions except those that
reward their rich and privileged benefactors. They are quite
candid about it, even acknowledging their mean spirit in
accomplishing it. Their leading strategist in Washington—
the same Grover Norquist—has famously said he wants to
shrink the government down to the size that it could be
drowned in a bathtub. More recently, in commenting on the
fiscal crisis in the states and its affect on schools and poor
people, Norquist said, "I hope one of them"—one of the
states—"goes bankrupt." So much for compassionate conservatism. But at least Norquist says what he means and
means what he says. The White House pursues the same
homicidal dream without saying so. Instead of shrinking
down the government, they're filling the bathtub with so
much debt that it floods the house, waterlogs the economy,
and washes away services for decades that have lifted millions of Americans out of destitution and into the middle-
class. And what happens once the public's property has been
flooded? Privatize it. Sell it at a discounted rate to the corporations. It is the most radical assault on the notion of one
nation, indivisible, that has occurred in our lifetime. I'll be
frank with you: I simply don't understand it—or the malice in
which it is steeped. Many people are nostalgic for a golden
age. These people seem to long for the Gilded Age. That I
can grasp. They measure America only by their place on the
material spectrum and they bask in the company of the new
corporate aristocracy, as privileged a class as we have seen
since the plantation owners of antebellum America and
the court of Louis IV. What I can't explain is the rage of the

counterrevolutionaries to dismantle every last brick of the social contract. At this advanced age I simply have to accept the fact that the tension between haves and have-nots is built into human psychology and society itself—it's ever with us. However, I'm just as puzzled as to why, with right-wing wrecking crews blasting away at social benefits once considered invulnerable, Democrats are fearful of being branded "class warriors" in a war the other side started and is determined to win. I don't get why conceding your opponent's premises and fighting on his turf isn't the sure-fire prescription for irrelevance and ultimately obsolescence. But I confess as well that I don't know how to resolve the social issues that have driven wedges into your ranks. And I don't know how to reconfigure Democratic politics to fit into an age of soundbites and polling dominated by a media oligarchy whose corporate journalists are neutered and whose right-wing publicists have no shame.

What I do know is this: While the social dislocations and meanness that galvanized progressives in the nineteenth century are resurgent, so is the vision of justice, fairness, and equality. That's a powerful combination if only there are people around to fight for it. The battle to renew democracy has enormous resources to call upon—and great precedents for inspiration. Consider the experience of James Bryce, who published *The Great Commonwealth* back in 1895 at the height of the First Gilded Age. Americans, Bryce said, "were hopeful and philanthropic." He saw first-hand the ills of that "dark and unlovely age," but he went on to say: " A hundred times I have been disheartened by the facts I was stating: a hundred times has the recollection of the abounding strength and vitality of the nation chased away those tremors."

What will it take to get back in the fight? Understanding the real interests and deep opinions of the American people is the first thing. And what are those? That a Social Security card is not a private portfolio statement but a membership ticket in a society where we all contribute to a common treasury so that none need face the indignities of poverty in old age without that help. That tax evasion is not a form of conserving investment capital but a brazen abandonment of responsibility to the country. That income inequality is not a sign of freedom-of-opportunity at work, because if it persists and grows, then unless you believe that some people are naturally born to ride and some to wear saddles, it's a sign that opportunity is less than equal. That self-interest is a great motivator for production and progress, but is amoral unless contained within the framework of community. That the rich have the right to buy more cars than anyone else, more homes, vacations, gadgets and gizmos, but they do not have the right to buy more democracy than anyone else. That public services, when privatized, serve only those who can afford them and weaken the sense that we all rise and fall together as "one nation, indivisible." That concentration in the production of goods may sometimes be useful and efficient, but monopoly over the dissemination of ideas is evil. That prosperity requires good wages and benefits for workers. And that our nation can no more survive as half democracy and half oligarchy than it could survive "half slave and half free"—and that keeping it from becoming all oligarchy is steady work—our work. Ideas have power—as long as they are not frozen in doctrine. But ideas need legs. The eight-hour day, the minimum wage, the conservation of natural resources and the protection of our air, water, and land, women's rights and civil rights, free trade unions, Social Security, and a civil service based on merit—all these were launched as citizen's movements and won the endorsement of the political class only after long struggles and in the face of bitter opposition and sneering attacks. It's just a fact: Democracy doesn't work without citizen activism and participation, starting at the community. Trickle-down politics doesn't work much better than trickle-down economics. It's also a fact that civilization happens because we don't leave things to other people. What's right and good doesn't come naturally. You have to stand up and fight for it—as if the cause depends on you, because it does. Allow yourself that conceit—to believe that the flame of democracy will never go out as long as there's one candle in your hand. So go for it. Never mind the odds. Remember what the progressives faced. Karl Rove isn't tougher than Mark Hanna was in his time and a hundred years from now some historian will be wondering how it was that Norquist and Company got away with it as long as they did—how they waged war almost unopposed on the infrastructure of social justice, on the arrangements that make life fair, on the mutual rights and responsibilities that offer opportunity, civil liberties, and a decent standard of living to the least among us.

"Democracy is not a lie"—I first learned that from Henry Demarest Lloyd, the progressive journalist whose book, *Wealth against Commonwealth*, laid open the Standard trust a century ago. Lloyd came to the conclusion to "Regenerate the individual is a half truth. The reorganization of the society which he makes and which makes him is the other part. The love of liberty *became* liberty in America by clothing itself in the complicated group of strengths known as the government of the United States." And it was then he said: "Democracy is not a lie. There live(s) in the body of the commonality unexhausted virtue and the ever-refreshed strength which can rise equal to any problems of progress. In the hope of tapping some reserve of their power of self-help," he said, "this story is told to the people."

This is your story—the progressive story of America.

Pass it on.

About the Contributors

WILLIAM GREIDER

William Greider is the national affairs correspondent for *The Nation*. He has been a political journalist for more than thirty-five years and is a prominent political journalist for newspapers, magazines, and television. A former *Rolling Stone* and *Washington Post* editor, he is the author of the national bestsellers *One World, Ready or Not, Secrets of the Temple, Who Will Tell the People* and, most recently, *The Soul of Capitalism*.

RALPH NEAS

Ralph G. Neas has been president of People for the American Way since January 2000. Previously, he served for fourteen years as Executive Director of the Leadership Council on Civil Rights where he was honored with their Hubert H. Humphrey Civil Rights Award. He has also received the Benjamin Hooks "Keeper of the Flame" award from the NAACP. Neas has been interviewed many times on ABC's *Nightline, CBS Sunday Morning,* NBC's *Today Show,* ABC's *This Week, The Newshour with Jim Lehrer* and National Public Radio. A native of Brookline, Massachusetts, he earned his B.A. from Notre Dame and his law degree from the University of Chicago.

DEB CALLAHAN

Deb Callahan has served as President of the League of Conservation Voters (LCV) since 1996 and has forged the organization into a potent bipartisan political force. Under her direction, the LCV embarked on such large-scale efforts as the Dirty Dozen campaigns, which are designed to defeat vulnerable anti-environmental candidates for Congress, and the Environmental Champions campaigns to support pro-environment candidates. A prominent voice for the environmental community, she appears regularly in print and on television, including such programs as *The Newshour with Jim Lehrer,* MSNBC's *Hardball,* Fox News's *The O'Reilly Factor* and on CNN.

WADE HENDERSON

Wade Henderson is the Executive Director of the Leadership Conference on Civil Rights (LCCR) and Counsel to the Leadership Conference on Civil Rights Education Fund. Currently he works on issues involving nationwide election reform, federal judicial appointments, public education reform, hate crimes, immigration and refugee policy, and human rights. Under his leadership, the LCCR has become one of the nation's most effective defenders of civil and human rights. Henderson is a graduate of Howard University and the Rutgers University School of Law.

KIM GANDY

Kim Gandy was elected President of the National Organization for Women on its 35th Anniversary, June 30, 2001, after serving as Executive Vice President since 1991. She chairs the NOW Foundation and the NOW Political Action Committee. A longtime activist, Gandy has served NOW at the local, state, and national levels since 1973. As Executive Vice President, she was responsible for NOW's legislative agenda and litigation docket, including *Scheidler v. NOW*, the landmark racketeering case against antiabortion terrorists. Gandy graduated from Louisiana Tech University in 1973 with a B.S. in mathematics and received her law degree from Loyala University School of Law in 1978.

JAMES K. GALBRAITH

James K. Galbraith teaches economics at the Lyndon B. Johnson School of Public Affairs and the University of Texas-Austin's Department of Government. He received a B.A. from Harvard University in 1974 and a Ph.D. in economics from Yale University in 1981. He is currently the Director of the University of Texas Inequality Project. He also serves as a Senior Scholar of the Levy Economics Institute and as chair of Economists Allied for Arms Reduction (ECAAR). He writes a column on economic and political issues for *The Texas Observer*.

ROBERT B. REICH

Robert B. Reich is a Maurice B. Hexter Professor of Social and Economic Policy at Brandeis University's Heller Graduate School. He has served in three federal administrations, most recently as Secretary of Labor under former President Bill Clinton. He has written nine books, including *The Work of Nations, Locked in the Cabinet*, and *The Future of Success*. His writings have appeared in *The New Yorker, The Atlantic*

Monthly, the *New York Times*, the *Washington Post*, and the *Wall Street Journal*, among others. Reich is co-founder and national editor of *The American Prospect*.

Barbara Ehrenreich

Barbara Ehrenreich is a contributing editor of *Harper's Magazine* and has written for *Time* magazine since 1990. Her articles, reviews, essays, and humor have appeared in a range of other publications, including the *New York Times Magazine*, the *Washington Post Magazine*, *Ms.*, *Esquire*, *The Atlantic Monthly*, *The Nation*, *The New Republic*, and *The Progressive*, as well as newspapers throughout the world. Ehrenreich is the author of *Nickel and Dimed: On (Not) Getting by in America*, and several other books. She has a Ph.D. in biology from the Rockefeller University and a B.A. from Reed College, and she has been a regular teaching fellow at the University of California-Berkeley Graduate School of Journalism.

Robert Kuttner

Robert Kuttner is founder and co-editor of *The American Prospect* and writes regularly for the magazine, often focusing on international and domestic economic policy. He is the author of five books and is a contributing columnist to *Business Week*'s "Economic Viewpoint." His weekly editorial column originates in *The Boston Globe* and is syndicated to about 20 major daily papers. Kuttner has taught at Brandeis University, Boston University, the University of Massachusetts and Harvard University's Institute of Politics. He was educated at Oberlin College, the University of California at Berkeley and the London School of Economics.

Earl Hadley

Earl Hadley is a researcher at the Institute for America's Future. His work has focused on education and economic growth. Before joining the Institute for America's Future, Earl worked as a researcher for Campbell-Kibler Associates, a research and evaluation firm focusing on education. He has also worked for the ERIC Clearinghouse on Urban Education, with the Director of Education at the National Urban League, and as Manager of Vassar College's Inter-Cultural Center. He has B.A. from Vassar College and an M.A. in Public Affairs from Princeton University.

Bracken Hendricks

Bracken Hendricks is the Director of the New Growth Initiative, a joint project of the Institute for America's Future and the Center on Wisconsin Strategy. The New Growth Initative is working to build labor alliances for energy efficiency and regional development that creates high-skill employment while providing environmental benefits. Hendricks has worked extensively at the intersection of labor and environmental issues as an economic analyst with the AFL-CIO. Hendricks served in the Clinton administration with Vice President Gore's National Partnership for Reinventing Government and as a Special Assistant to the Department of Commerce's National Oceanic and Atmospheric Administration. Hendricks holds an M.A. in Public Policy and Urban Planning from Harvard University's John F. Kennedy School of Government.

Benjamin Barber

Benjamin Barber is the Gershon and Carol Kekst Professor

of Civil Society at the University of Maryland and a principal of The Democracy Collective. He consults regularly with political and civic leaders in the U.S. and Europe, including Governor James McGreevey of New Jersey, former President Bill Clinton, former Vice President Al Gore, former Senator Bill Bradley and President Roman Herzog of Germany. He writes frequently for *Harper's Magazine*, the *New York Times*, *The Atlantic*, and *The Nation*, among others. He holds a certificate from the London School of Economics and Political Science and an M.A. and Doctorate from Harvard University. He is currently working on the CivWorld Global Citizens Campaign and the Agora Coalition Initiative on Smart Growth and Sprawl.

TOM ANDREWS

Tom Andrews is National Director of Win Without War, a coalition of thirty-two groups, including the NAACP and the Sierra Club, opposing the U.S. attack on Iraq. Widely respected as an excellent grassroots organizer, Andrews has advocated for disabled rights, and gun control, opponents to nuclear-waste storage. Along the way, he served in the Maine Legislature and U.S. Congress. Ralph Nader once called him "the most principled politician I have ever met." He currently serves on the advisory board to Peace Action Maine. Andrews founded New Economy Communications in 1988 to encourage broad coverage and greater understanding of economic issues.

WILLIAM S. LERACH

William S. Lerach is a partner in Milberg Weiss Bershad

Hynes & Lerach, LLP, and is widely recognized as one of the leading securities lawyers in the U.S. Lerach is a member of the American Bar Association Litigation Section's Committee on Class Actions and Derivative Skills, and has been involved in many of the largest and highest profile securities class action and corporate derivative suits in recent years, including Enron, Dynegy, Qwest, and WorldCom. He is a member of the Editorial Board of *Class Action Reports* and frequently lectures on class and derivative actions, accountants' liability, and attorneys' fees. He is also a member of the American Law Institute faculty on Federal and State Class Action Litigation. Lerach was honored by former President Clinton who appointed him a member of the United States Holocaust Memorial Council.

MILES RAPOPORT

Miles Rapoport, a leading authority on democracy reform issues, has served as president of Demos: A Network for Ideas and Action, since 2001. Demos is a nonpartisan organization based in New York City, which seeks to strengthen U.S. democracy and broaden economic opportunity. Rapoport served for ten years in the Connecticut legislature before being elected Secretary of the State in 1994. He is also the founder of Northeast Action, a leading political reform organization in New England, and was formerly the Executive Director of DemocracyWorks, a Hartford-based democracy reform organization he founded in 1999.

JEFF BLODGETT

Jeff Blodgett is the Executive Director of Wellstone Action, an organization formed to carry on the work of U.S. Senator Paul Wellstone and his wife, Sheila Wellstone. Blodgett spent thirteen years as a senior aide, advisor, and campaign manager to Senator Wellstone. He ran all three of the senator's election campaigns. Blodgett also has extensive experience in nonprofit political advocacy. He started and ran The Alliance Project, a national effort to increase the advocacy ability of organizations and individuals supporting alcohol and drug addiction treatment and recovery. In 1997, Blodgett was awarded a Bush Leadership Fellowship that allowed him to receive his Masters of Public Administration degree at Harvard University's Kennedy School of Government.

John Nichols

John Nichols, *The Nation*'s Washington correspondent, has covered progressive politics and activism in the United States and abroad for more than a decade. Formerly a writer and editor for the Toledo *Blade* and Pittsburgh *Post-Gazette* newspapers, he is now editorial page editor for the *Capital Times* in Madison, Wisconsin. He has covered electoral politics for *The Progressive* for a number of years. His articles have appeared in the *New York Times*, the Chicago *Tribune,* and dozens of other newspapers. Nichols has covered four presidential elections in the United States, along with elections and political activism in Britain, Ireland, Israel, India, Palestine, El Salvador, Jamaica, and South Africa. He is the author, with Robert W. McChesney, of *It's the Media, Stupid,* and *Jews for Buchanan,* on the 2000 presidential election.

Robert W. McChesney

Robert W. McChesney is Research Professor in the Institute of Communications Research and the Graduate School of Library and Information Science at the University of Illinois at Urbana-Champaign. In 2002 he co-founded the Illinois Initiative on Global Information and Communication Policy. McChesney also hosts the *Media Matters* weekly radio program. From 1988 to 1998 he was on the Journalism and Mass Communication faculty at the University of Wisconsin-Madison. McChesney earned his Ph.D. in communications at the University of Washington in 1989. His work concentrates on the history and political economy of communication, emphasizing the role media play in democratic and capitalist societies. McCheasney has written numerous books and journal articles.

Joel Rogers

Joel Rogers is a contributing editor at *The Nation* and *Boston Review*. He is the director of the Center on Wisconsin Strategy and the John D. MacArthur Professor of Law, Political Science, and Sociology at UW-Madison. Rogers has written widely on American politics and public policy, political theory, and U.S. and comparative industrial relations. His most recent books are *Working Capital: Using the Power of Labor's Pensions* (2001); *America's Forgotten Majority: Why the White Working Class Still Matters* (2000); *What Workers Want* (1999); and *Metro Futures: Economic Solutions for the Cities and their Suburbs* (1999). Rogers writes a weekly "Sustaining Wisconsin" column for the *Capital Times*. A MacArthur Foundation fellow and a longtime social activist,

Rogers was identified by *Newsweek* as one of the 100 Americans most likely to affect U.S. politics and culture in the twenty-first century.

DANNY GOLDBERG

Danny Goldberg, Chairman and CEO of the independent record company Artemis Records, and President and CEO of Sheridan Square Entertainment, is one of the most socially active music business executives. In 1980, Goldberg co-produced and co-directed the rock documentary feature, *No Nukes*. In 1984, he co-produced MTV's first voter registration TV commercials, and in 1986, he produced the Rock Against Drugs TV commercials for MTV. Goldberg is on the Board of Directors and Executive Committee of the New York Civil Liberties Union and is the President of the ACLU Foundation of Southern California. In that capacity and as a spokesman for the music business, he has appeared on the *Today Show, CBS Morning News, CNN Crossfire* and the *Charlie Rose Show*. In recent years, Goldberg has written about civil liberties, politics and the music business for the *Los Angeles Times, New York Daily News, Newsday, The Nation, The American Prospect, Inside.com*, and *Tikkun*. Goldberg also serves on the Board of Directors of The Nation Institute, Rock the Vote, The Creative Coalition, The Abraham Fund, and Jewish Television Network.

KATRINA VANDEN HEUVEL

Katrina vanden Heuvel is editor of *The Nation*. She is the co-author of *Voices of Glasnost: Interviews with Gorbachev's Reformers* and editor of the anthologies, *The Nation:*

1865–1990, The Best of The Nation: Selections from the Independent Magazine of Politics and Culture, and the collection *A Just Response: The Nation on Terrorism, Democracy and September 11, 2001.*

She is a frequent commentator on American and international politics on CNN and MSNBC. Katrina vanden Heuvel also writes about American and Russian politics. Her editorials and articles have appeared in the *Washington Post,* the *Los Angeles Times,* the *New York Times* and the *Boston Globe.*

She is a recipient of Planned Parenthood's Maggie Award for her article, "Right-to-Lifers Hit Russia." The special issue she conceived and edited, "Gorbachev's Soviet Union," was awarded New York University's 1988 Olive Branch Award.

She has received awards for public service from numerous groups, including The Liberty Hill Foundation, The Correctional Association and The Association for American-Russian Women. Katrina vanden Heuvel is a member of The Council on Foreign Relations and The Century Association and serves on the board of The Institute for Women's Policy Research, The Arca Foundation, The Institute for Policy Studies, The World Policy Institute, The Correctional Association of New York and The Franklin and Eleanor Roosevelt Institute.

ROBERT L. BOROSAGE

Robert L. Borosage is co-director of the Campaign for America's Future. Previously, Borosage founded and directed the Campaign for New Priorities, a nonprofit organization calling for post-Cold War reinvestment in America. Borosage writes for publications including the *New York Times*, the *Washington Post*, the *Los Angeles Times*, the

Philadelphia Inquirer, and *The Nation*. He is a frequent commentator for television and radio, including the *PBS Newshour, Fox Morning News,* National Public Radio, C-SPAN, and Pacifica Radio. In 1988, he was Senior Issues Advisor to the presidential campaign of Reverend Jesse Jackson. He has also served as an issues advisor to many progressive political campaigns, including those of senators Carol Moseley Braun, Barbara Boxer, and Paul Wellstone. Borosage is a graduate of Yale Law School, and holds a Masters Degree in International Relations from George Washington University.

Gloria Totten

Gloria Totten took the helm as Executive Director of Progressive Majority, a political action committee, in May 2001. Prior to that, she served as Political Director for the National Abortion and Reproductive Rights Action League (NARAL). At NARAL, she ran a multi-million dollar department budget and was responsible for all the electoral and political organizing work, as well as managing NARAL's 27 state affiliates. While there, Totten also worked to develop the organization's first nationwide pro-choice voter file, which consisted of 2.9 million pro-choice identified voters in 2000. She also devised all of NARAL's advocacy campaigns, including numerous ballot initiative campaigns, legislative battles and the Stop Ashcroft! Campaign in 2001. She volunteers at My Sister's Place, a battered women's shelter in Washington, DC, and currently serves on the Boards of Directors for the Bridge Builders Fund and the Ballot Initiative Strategy Center.

REPRESENTATIVE JAN SCHAKOWSKY

Rep. Jan D. Schakowsky was elected to represent Illinois' Ninth Congressional District in 1998 after serving for eight years in the Illinois State Assembly. Schakowsky serves on the House Democratic Leadership team as Chief Deputy Whip, and is a member of the Energy and Commerce Committee, where she is working to accomplish her top priority in Congress: providing universal health care coverage for all Americans. A citizen advocate, grassroots organizer, and elected public official, she has fought throughout her career for economic and social justice and improved quality of life for all, for an end to violence against women, and for a national investment in health care, public education, and housing needs. She graduated from the University of Illinois in 1965 with a B.S. in Elementary Education.

THE REVEREND JESSE L. JACKSON

The Reverend Jesse Jackson, Sr., President and founder of the Rainbow/Push Coalition, is one of America's foremost political figures. Over the past thirty years he has played a pivotal role in virtually every movement for empowerment, peace, civil rights, gender equality, and economic and social justice. Rev. Jackson has been called the "conscience of the nation" and "the great unifier," challenging America to establish just and humane priorities. He is known for bringing people together across lines of race, class, gender and belief. He has been a major force in the American labor movement, as well, working with unions to organize workers and mediate labor disputes. He attended the University of Illinois on a football scholarship and later transferred to North Carolina

Agricultural & Technical State University. He attended Chicago Theological Seminary until he joined the civil rights movement full time in 1965.

BILL MOYERS

Bill Moyers had been a print journalist, ordained Baptist minister, press secretary to President Lyndon Johnson and newspaper publisher before coming to television in 1970. During his twenty-five years in broadcasting he has pursued a broad spectrum of journalism. In 1986, Moyers formed Public Affairs Television, Inc., with his wife and partner, Judith. This independent production company has produced more than 300 hours of programming. In 2002, Moyers launched the weekly PBS series *Now with Bill Moyers*. A survey of television critics by Television Quarterly placed Moyers among the ten journalists who have had the most influence on television news. His work has been recognized with more than thirty Emmy Awards. He was elected to the Television Hall of Fame in 1995, and a year later received the Charles Frankel Prize form the National Endowment for the Humanities "for outstanding contributions to American cultural life."

Permissions

"Rolling Back the 20th Century" by William Greider. Reprinted with permission of *The Nation* © 2003 *The Nation*. • "The War Against Women" by Kim Gandy © 2003 by Kim Gandy. • "Rolling Back Basic Rights" by Wade Henderson © 2003 by Wade Henderson. • "Trashing the Environment" by Deb Callahan © 2003 by Deb Callahan. • "Packing the Courts" by Ralph G. Neas © 2003 by Ralph G. Neas. • "Full Economic Recovery and Full Employment" by James K. Galbraith © 2003 by James K. Galbraith. • "A Program for a New Majority" by Robert B. Reich © 2003 by Robert B. Reich. • "Empowering Working People" by Barbara Ehrenreich © 2003 by Barbara Ehrenreich. • "Healthcare—the Logic of Radical Reform" by Robert Kuttner © 2003 by Robert Kuttner. • "America's Commitment to Education" by Robert L. Borosage and Earl Hadley © 2003 by Robert L. Borosage and Earl Hadley. • "The Apollo Initiative" by Bracken Hendricks © 2003 by Bracken Hendricks. • "A Real Security Agenda" by Benjamin Barber © 2003 by Ben Barber. • "Security in a Changed World" by Tom Andrews © 2003 by Tom Andrews. • "America Law" by William S. Lerach © 2003 by William S. Lerach. • "Seizing the Continuing Moment for Democracy Reform" by Miles Rapoport © 2003 by Miles Rapoport. • "The Winning Ways of Paul Wellstone" by Jeff Blodgett © 2003 by Jeff Blodgett. • "Up in Flames" by John Nichols and Robert McChesney. Reprinted with permission of *The Nation* © 2003 *The Nation*. • "Devolve This!" by Joel Rogers © 2003 by Joel Rogers. • "Youth Vote in 2004" by Danny Goldberg © 2003 by Danny Goldberg. • "Building to Win" by Katrina vanden Heuvel © 2003 by Katrina vanden Heuvel. • "Growing a Progressive Majority" by Gloria Totten © 2003 by Gloria Totten. • "Organize, Don't Agonize" by Rep. Jan Schakowsky © 2003 by Rep. Jan Schakowsky. • "Bring the Family Together" by The Rev. Jesse L. Jackson © 2003 by Rev. Jesse L. Jackson. • "The Acceptance of America's Future Lifetime Leadership Award" by Bill Moyers © 2003 by Bill Moyers.